portals

Entering Your Neighbor's World

portals

Entering Your Neighbor's World

GLENN SUNSHINE

Every Square Inch Publishing
Newington, CT 06111

Published by Every Square Inch Publishing
Newington, Connecticut 06111-4344
esquareinch@gmail.com

ISBN 978-0-9838051-5-1

For additional resources and information on this and other
titles by this author, visit our website at esquareinch.com.

This book is dedicated to the memory of
Charles W. Colson, friend and mentor,
who suggested I write it, and to all the Centurions
past and present, for their hard work and
dedication to worldview ministry.

Table of Contents

Acknowledgements

Too many people have contributed to my understanding of worldviews for me to properly thank all of them here. Some, however, deserve special mention for this particular project:

- Andrew Bieszad, for his expertise on Islam;

- Art Lindsley, for his expertise on the New Age Movement;

- Dave Gilbert for the cover design;

- Ken Boa for help with the title and much else;

- Paul Marks, John Nunnikhoven, Elizabeth Sunshine, Henry and Janet Von Wodtke, and Martha Anderson for editorial help.

Needless to say, any errors or omissions in the book are my responsibility, not theirs.

Introduction

This book is a very brief survey of the major worldviews in contemporary American society. Some of these will be very familiar to you; others less so, but all of them are helping to shape Western culture and ideas. If you want to understand your neighbors and communicate effectively with them, it pays to understand their basic ideas about the world, because those ideas may be very different from your own.

What is a Worldview?

Before we go any further, we should stop for a moment to define the word, "worldview." Your worldview is how you see the world and your place in it. It is the operating system your mind uses to make sense of the world, the mental eyeglasses you use to bring the world around you into clear mental focus. Many of these ideas are held unconsciously, though some of them come from conscious reflection and choice. But even those who do not think much about these things have a worldview. Quite simply, it is impossible to live in or interact with the world without one, since your worldview determines what you think about what is possible, what is true, what is right, what is wrong, what "makes sense," even what is real. In other words, your worldview sets the boundaries of the world you live in.

People who study worldviews have taken a variety of approaches to try to analyze and define what makes up a worldview. For example, I argue in *Why You Think the Way You Do* (Zondervan, 2009) that a worldview includes answers to the basic philosophical questions of what is real (metaphysics), what is true (epistemology), and what is right and wrong (ethics), along with "higher level" questions about human origins, the meaning of life, etc. James Sire has a different but overlapping set of questions in *The Universe Next Door* (InterVarsity Press, fourth edition, 2004). Ravi Zacharias summarizes worldviews under four headings: origins, meaning, morality, and destiny (*This We Believe*, Zondervan, 2000).

For this book, we will use a set of four questions outlined by Charles W. Colson in *How Now Shall We Live?* (Tyndale House, 1999). Colson sidesteps to some extent the problem of listing all the elements of a worldview, and instead argues that when all is said and done, the worldview must answer four fundamental questions: where did I come from? What is wrong with the world? Is there a solution? What is my purpose? These correspond to the basic Christian themes of Creation, Fall, Redemption, and Restoration, though their implications go well beyond the usual theological discussions of these topics. And sooner or later, even non-Christian worldviews need to deal with these issues.

In some ways, Colson sneaks a fifth question in the back door: what is truth and can we know it? Since this question provides a framework for answering the other questions, however, we will follow Colson's lead and deal with differing ideas of truth in the introductory material to each worldview, not as one of the fundamental questions.

Categorizing Worldviews

Despite the many ways of analyzing worldviews, most people who deal with the subject are in general agreement about the main worldviews present in the world today. In this book, we will deal with seven broad worldview categories, with some sub-systems as well.

- **Historic Christianity**. This is the worldview taught in the Christian Bible as it has been interpreted within the broad Christian tradition—Eastern Orthodox, Roman Catholic, and Protestant—for the past two millennia. Rather than being simply a religion, Christianity is a worldview because it answers all the basic worldview questions, and like any worldview, it encompasses all of life.
- **Secular Naturalism**. This worldview starts with the assumption that matter and energy are all that exist and follows the consequences out from there. There are several varieties of secular naturalism, including *nihilism*, and *existentialism*. We will focus here on the most common version of secular naturalism in contemporary society which comes from *scientism*, the idea that science and science alone, operating out of secular naturalist assumptions, is the only legitimate way of finding truth.
- **Postmodernism**. This worldview is particularly difficult to define clearly, but is based on the premise that absolute truth does not exist and that everything we think of as reality is simply a social construct, that is, that it reflects what

society believes to be true rather than what is actually real. Although there are a bewildering range of views within postmodernism, in this chapter we will focus on an ideological variety that has had an enormous political and social impact in America.

- **Islam**. There are a variety of forms of Islam, but as a worldview, Islam has a number of common ideas at its core that transcend the sectarian divides within the religion. Islam is primarily focused on proper practice, and so divisions tend to be about what you do rather than what you think. Since our focus here is on worldview, we will focus on what the Quran—the source of truth within Islam—teaches about the four basic questions. Do all Muslims accept these answers? No, no more than all Christians follow a biblical worldview. But as a worldview, these are the answers offered by devout Muslims across the board.

- **Eastern Religions**. This is a very large and diverse category. A number of common worldview ideas lie behind most Eastern religions, though how these ideas work themselves out varies considerably. Here, we will look at the worldview that supports these religions, noting some of the nuances in the answers to the questions offered by major forms of Hinduism, Buddhism, and Taoism.

- **New Age Movement**. This is frequently seen as a sub-category of Eastern thought, but it is different on a number of fronts. It combines elements of secular naturalism and postmodernism with Eastern religions and a wide range of other belief systems as well to produce an eclectic, individualized vision of spirituality (generally separated from religion) with the hope of bringing a New Age of peace and harmony to the world. As a result, it deserves a separate treatment.

- **Gaian Worldview**. The Gaian worldview exists in several different forms, some based on science and some on various kinds of spirituality. As a result, it can fit under several different categories, including secular naturalism, postmodernism or the New Age, but given the common answers to the worldview questions found in all varieties of this worldview, it is worth treating it separately. This worldview sees the Earth and all the creatures that live on it as a single unified system, possibly even a living being itself. Its primary concern is for the health of the environment, which it sees as being threatened by human action. Salvation in this system is found by taking action to protect the planet (not necessarily to protect humanity) from a pending ecological apocalypse.

How to Use This Book

The summaries in the following chapters are not exhaustive or definitive, but are intended simply as general introduction to key themes in each worldview and to point out some of the implications of the ideas. The goal is to give you an orientation to the worldviews to enable you to better understand the people around you and to communicate with them more effectively.

16

In an evangelistic context, worldview discussions are most useful as part of what some have called "pre-evangelism," that is, conversations intended to help the person open up to hearing the Gospel. The rule you have to keep in mind here is that *people are not going to be interested in what you have until they're dissatisfied with what they have.* This holds true in virtually any evangelistic context, but for our purposes here, one of the most effective ways to use worldviews in evangelism is to prompt dissatisfaction with the individual's current worldview. So how do you do this? As Colson argues, only the biblical worldview found in historic Christianity is true (that is, it is the only one that conforms to reality) and as a result, it is the only worldview which is fully livable. Every other worldview is in tension with reality at some point(s), and the object in worldview evangelism is to help the individual recognize that tension. In other words, we need to guide them to see where their worldview breaks down, either because it is inconsistent with itself or because it does not conform to reality or because it is simply impossible to live consistently with its premises. For example, many people will argue that there is no such thing as right and wrong, and yet they will complain when they are cheated, mistreated, or even simply cut off in traffic. But if there is no such thing as right and wrong, how can you complain about "wrongs" being done to you? By pointing out these inconsistencies, you begin to show that the worldview simply does not work. The late Francis Schaeffer was a master at this, and I highly recommend his books, which include many examples of this kind of conversation.

Keep in mind, however, that the object is to help the person think clearly through their ideas, not to play "gotcha" with them. The conversation must be intended

to honor the person you are talking to and to le[a]
that person thinks, not what these summaries s[a]
she should think. People are often not very consi[stent] in
their thinking: they often pick and choose what they
like from different worldviews, not realizing the
inconsistencies that this introduces to their thinking. In
other words, do *not* assume that any particular
individual will have a consistent worldview or will line
up 100% under one of these categories. So in
conversations with people about their worldviews, ask
questions about what they think and why. Further, it
helps to understand where the ideas of the different
worldviews lead, but do not assume that just because
someone has adopted a worldview, he or she will
realize all of its implications. So again, ask questions
about whether or not the person accepts the
consequences of their ideas, and if not, ask why. The
focus must always be on the individual, not on systems
or worldview categories.

With that in mind, we turn first to historic
Christianity.

1—Historic Christianity

Christianity is a worldview. It provides a comprehensive framework for understanding reality based on ideas found in the Bible. For historic Christianity, biblical teaching is the foundation for how we approach all of life.

For anyone who knows anything about Christianity, the idea that there is one Christian worldview or one worldview found in the Bible raises an immediate question: given the diversity of theological traditions drawn from the Bible—Catholic, Eastern Orthodox, Protestants, Pentecostals, Evangelicals, Fundamentalists, the list goes on and on—can we really talk about *the* biblical worldview? Aren't there many biblical worldviews? While there are many ways of interpreting the Bible, the underlying worldview of any interpretation that takes the Bible seriously is very consistent. In other words, the Bible, taken on its own terms, presents a coherent worldview that is the core of historic Christianity in all its varieties.

The biblical worldview has decisively shaped Western civilization even in areas that are not normally considered religious, including some that are frequently believed to be hostile to religion. Western science, technology, economics, politics, ideas of freedom and human rights, education, ideas about love, marriage and family, all are consequences of the biblical worldview.

To understand why, consider the basic Christian doctrines that God is the creator of the universe and that

18

humanity is made in His image. These ideas have several important implications:

- Since God is rational, He made a rational universe, and since we are made in His image, we can understand that universe. Thus investigation of the way the world really works—thinking God's thoughts after Him—is an act of worship. This was an important motivation for nearly all the scientists in the Western tradition through Isaac Newton and beyond.

- Since God created all things, everything is of interest to Him. The biblical worldview argues that all truth—that which corresponds to reality—is God's truth, and thus sees all areas of learning as worthwhile. This is why churches have always founded schools from the early centuries AD to today.

- Since God is a creator, so are we. The church has historically been a major patron and inspiration for the visual arts, architecture, music, and literature. Christianity has also provided a rich source of themes and images for secular art as well.

- Because human dignity in the biblical worldview is founded on the image of God which all people share, the Western world developed ideas of freedom, civil rights and equality. Thus, for example, slavery disappeared in medieval Europe, and medieval theologians articulated the ideas of inalienable rights that would find their way into the Declaration of Independence.

- Concern about human dignity led to the development and deployment of technologies to eliminate drudgery from work. Labor itself was seen as a positive good for the first time in human history.
- Concern about human dignity also led churches to found hospitals and orphanages around the world.

These observations immediately lead to the objection that Christians have not actually lived up to these ideals, and that Christians are in fact hypocritical. However, the very fact that we see these things as ideals demonstrates the Christian influence on culture: none of these were present in the Greco-Roman world, and only emerged in the West as a result of the growing influence of Christian theology. Further, failure to live up to a set of ideals does not invalidate those ideals. Is it fair to judge a religion or worldview on the basis of people who do not live consistently with it?

Since Christianity claims to have a comprehensive picture of how the world works and how we fit into it, one that corresponds with reality in a way no other worldview does, what are the key elements of the biblical worldview? How does Christianity address the four major worldview questions?

Question 1: Where Did I Come From?

Human beings are a special creation of God, made in His image.

Christians differ on such issues as the age of the Earth and the timing and processes involved in our origins, but the idea that we are made in the image of God is fundamental to the biblical worldview and to the biblical understanding of what it means to be human. The Bible places a premium on human life because we are made in God's image (Gen. 9:6). And historically, the ideas of human equality and human rights were developed by Christian thinkers who were working out the implications of what it means to be made in the image of God.

But what is the image of God? How does it show itself in our lives? Theologians and biblical scholars have identified a number of elements of the image of God that highlight our unique place in the creation.

- Because God is rational, we are *rational*. Although we cannot begin to understand everything that God has done, we can think God's thoughts after Him, analyze, learn, and develop our understanding of the world and our place in it.
- Because God is moral, we are *moral*. We know innately that there is right and wrong, and we judge ourselves and others on the basis of whether or not we do the things we believe are right.
- Because God is spirit, we are *spiritual*. We are not just a complex biochemical machine. There is a non-physical part of us, and that part is designed for fellowship with God.
- Because God is Trinity, He is relational and we are *relational*. God exists as a community of persons, and we too are made to connect with God and with each other. God's explanation for the creation of Eve in the Garden of Eden was, "it is not good for the man to be alone" (Gen. 2:18)—the only thing in all of creation God

pronounced "not good." We are made for relationships.

- Because God works, we **work**. God worked in the Creation, and humanity was given work in the Garden of Eden even prior to sin. This was both intellectual or creative work (naming the animals, Gen. 2:19) and production (tending the Garden, Gen. 2:15). We are not made to be idle but to contribute meaningfully to the development of culture.

- Because God is sovereign, we have **authority**. In the ancient Near East, where the Bible was written, the image of a god was that god's official regent or representative on Earth. In Gen. 1:26, being made in the image of God is associated with our role as "rulers" over the creation. At the same time, the Bible is clear that the earth is the Lord's (e.g. Ps. 24:1), not ours, so our authority is the authority of a steward, not an owner. We are to do our work in a way that honors God and His creation, and does not destroy it.

Most importantly, the image of God does not depend on what we can or cannot do, but on who we are. It does not change with physical, mental or emotional disabilities and it stays with us throughout our lives from beginning to end. Each of us is unique and uniquely valuable before God, precious and of inestimable worth.

Question 2: What is Wrong with the World?

Human choice is responsible for sin and suffering in the world.

God created humanity with the capacity to love Him, but love cannot be coerced. It must be freely given or it is not love. As a result, God gave humanity free will so we could choose whether or not to love Him, as shown by obeying Him. The choice Adam and Eve were given was either to enjoy the Garden of Eden, except for one tree, or to eat from that tree and die. Ultimately, Adam and Eve decided not to trust that God had their best interests at heart, and decided they would rather challenge His authority than submit to it. As a result, the image of God, that unique source of human dignity, was marred (though not completely lost) for them and all of their descendants.

The first result of sin was *alienation from God* (Gen. 3:8): Adam tried to avoid God when he knew He was near. But God sought Adam out, and Adam then showed that he also experienced *alienation from himself* as he tried to avoid responsibility for his actions by blaming Eve and God for giving her to him (Gen. 3:12). This also showed that Adam and Eve were experiencing *alienation from each other*, and in a particularly devastating way: it divided husband and wife and thus damaged the core of the family, the building block of society and the place where the image of God was uniquely to be seen (Gen.1:27). Finally, Adam and Eve experienced *alienation from nature* (Gen. 3:16-19), as Eve would give birth in pain and Adam's work would turn to drudgery, with the land itself fighting against him. Since Adam was God's regent on earth, his disobedience to God by trying to usurp authority from the One who truly ruled creation resulted in the physical universe itself not being able to fulfill its intended purposes (Rom. 8:20-22).

All evil in this world is ultimately a consequence of Adam's sin and the Fall. We have inherited a propensity to sin ("original sin") from our first parents, and we inevitably disobey God both through being deceived (as did Eve) and through acting knowingly and intentionally (as did Adam). We do not desire the right things, and so we do not do the right things. Even when we deliberately try to deny the validity of God's instructions for how to live and set up our own version of morality, we cannot live consistently with it. As a result, we have no right to complain about being innocent victims of the evil in the world. The simple fact is, we contribute to that evil ourselves. As G. K. Chesterton once said, original sin is the only doctrine of philosophy empirically verified by 35 centuries of recorded human history.

Christianity is unique in its idea of original sin. All other religions and worldviews place the reason for evil elsewhere, never as a taint in human nature itself. No worldview that does not have grace at its center can have a doctrine of original sin. And grace is at the center of Adam and Eve's story as well: although God told Adam and Eve they would die on the day they ate from the tree, they did not. But something else did: God provided them with animal skins to cover their nakedness and shame, and thus an animal was sacrificed for them. This provision of a substitute points ahead to the biblical solution to the problem of evil.

Question 3: Is There a Solution?

Through Christ's death and resurrection, God has provided the solution to all that is wrong with the world.

The Bible teaches that the most important attribute of God is His holiness, which among other things means that He is completely separate from sin and evil and cannot tolerate its presence. God's very character demands that He judge sin. Since God is infinitely holy, and even at our best, we can only offer finite holiness, the gap between God and humanity is infinite and the payment to bridge the gap created by our sins must be equally infinite. As a result, there is no way human beings can ever earn their way to forgiveness. But at the same time, God loves us and wants a relationship with us. So what we could not do for ourselves, God did for us by sending His Son, the eternal second person in the Trinity, to become human, to live a sinless life on our behalf, and to die unjustly on the cross, taking on Himself the penalty that is due to us for our sin. He then rose from the dead, providing the possibility of new life for us. In essence, He offers an exchange: Jesus will take the penalty for our sins on the cross, and we in exchange can take His righteousness and receive His resurrection life as our own. If we are humble enough to accept this offer on faith, we can obtain forgiveness of our sins and spend eternity with God in heaven.

So Christ's death on the cross reconciles us with God, ending the alienation that separates us from Him. But it does more than that. It also is the foundation for reconciled relationships with each other, as we recognize that all people (starting with ourselves) are sinners, and within the community of faith we are all saved by one Lord, serve one Master, and have new life through the same resurrection. There is thus no ground for pride, division, recriminations—we have the potential now to live in unity whatever our background. Knowing that our needs have all been met by Christ, we can now reach out to serve those around us selflessly and without fear, seeking to meet their needs as freely as Christ met ours.

Within ourselves, although we will continue to struggle with sin, we know that our victory and our deliverance from sin are ultimately secure, thanks to our position in Christ. We no longer need to be paralyzed by guilt or to try to blame others or find an excuse for our misbehavior. The Gospel begins with a sober, hard-hitting assessment of our guilt, but ends with forgiveness and reconciliation, so our failures need not cripple us. We should instead act with true humility, extending grace to others rather than trying to justify ourselves. There is, of course, a process involved. Our behavior and our attitudes are not transformed instantly to the new realities that are ours in Christ, but we should be constantly striving, growing, and maturing in Him so that our thoughts, words, and actions become progressively more in line with Christ's.

But reconciliation with God, our neighbor, and ourselves does not exhaust the work of Christ's death and resurrection. The work of Christ also provides the foundation for our reconciliation with the created order. Our sin affected the earth's physical environment since we were intended to be God's regents here. But God's love extends to the whole world (Greek *cosmos*, the created order) according to John 3:16, and Christ's death and resurrection provide redemption not just for humanity, but for all that was marred with humanity's fall. The results are not immediate, and the ultimate redemption of the earth will not take place until we ourselves experience the fullness of our redemption at Christ's second coming, when He will usher in a new heaven and new earth. In the meantime, God's call to us to be His stewards has not been rescinded. We are to take up once again our stewardship of the earth, taking care of it under God's direction and developing our resources and culture to give honor back to the God who entrusted the world to us and gave us our talents and creativity.

Question 4: What is My Purpose?

My purpose is to build God's kingdom by doing His will and working to restore fallen society.

God has given His people two great tasks. The first, known as the Great Commission, is to make disciples, baptizing them in the name of the Father and of the Son, and of the Holy Spirit, and teaching them to obey all that Jesus has commanded (Matt. 28:19-20). This is often misunderstood as simply preaching salvation through accepting Jesus as your savior. While this is an important component of the Gospel, it is not enough. We also need to teach repentance and the Lordship of Christ. In the Great Commission, Jesus did not tell us to make converts or to get people to "make a decision" for Him; He told us to make disciples who obey Him in all things. The Gospel is the Gospel of the Kingdom (Matt. 24:14), the place where Christ reigns. Those who claim to be His must therefore live under His authority, doing His will, and promoting His rule to others by calling them into the Kingdom and teaching them to obey Him. True evangelism is thus focused on making disciples who accept the Lordship of Christ and who are taught to grow in their knowledge and obedience to Him.

28

The second task God has given us is the cultural mandate, sometimes called the cultural commission. Christ is not only the Lord of our salvation or our lives; He is Lord of all—all creation, all culture, all relationships, all spheres of human life and activity, everything. As we build His kingdom, we need to bring the values of the Kingdom to bear in our families, our jobs and businesses, and our leisure. But the cultural mandate goes beyond questions of morals and values. We need to engage in our intellectual and physical labor as God's stewards, recognizing that there is no area of life in which God is not interested. This means that there is no division between the sacred and the secular in the biblical worldview. Being a missionary is no more "holy" a calling than being a banker, a businessman, a musician in a jazz band, an athlete, a politician, or a trash collector. All are legitimate callings from God and all can be done as an act of worship and service to our Creator. As Martin Luther said, the workplace is an altar. We need to do our jobs recognizing that we are working for God first, not our employer.

Our work is part of the renewal of God's call to Adam and Eve to be His stewards in the world by building culture through wise development of the physical and creative resources He has placed at our disposal. This means, however, that in our building of culture we must also be concerned about the environment. While we do not place ultimate value on ecological issues—human beings are more valuable than animals, for example, since we are created in the image of God and the animals are not—nonetheless, as stewards we are caretakers of creation for God. We are to tend it, nurture it, and develop it wisely, not wastefully or wantonly, with the goal of passing down a better tended and developed world to our children we received from our parents.

We are also to work ~~for restored~~ relationships between people. Jesus tells us that the peacemakers are blessed (Matt. 5:19). The Hebrew concept of peace is more than simply the absence of conflict; it means everything that is needed for human flourishing. Christians should be—and have been—at the forefront of efforts to reconcile racial differences, ethnic conflict, and any other kind of division that disrupts our unity as men and women made in the image of God.

In building Christ's kingdom, then, we build culture through wise, non-exploitive, use of resources; we live in harmonious relations with other people, ~~working for social justice~~; the dignity and value of our work is affirmed; and we find ourselves living for higher and greater purposes than our self-gratification. And this is the Kingdom to which we invite people in our evangelism, and what it means to teach people to obey all that Christ commands.

2—Secular Naturalism

Secular naturalism begins with the assumption that the only things that exist in the universe are matter and energy. This assumption generally leads to *scientism*, the belief that the best (and only) route to truth is via the scientific method. Scientism commonly leads to disdain for anyone who suggests moral limits on what kinds of scientific or technological research should be permitted and in the tendency to view knowledge of the natural world as the only truth, with everything else being opinion, preference, prejudice, or faith (an approach sometimes called the *fact/faith distinction*). Of course, the basic premise of scientism is not itself scientifically verifiable, which makes the idea itself a matter of faith, not "fact."

In terms of ideas about God, in its pure form secular naturalism is atheistic, though *pantheism* (the idea that the universe itself is god) is a possibility as well, as long as god is understood as impersonal and is effectively reduced to a source of feelings of transcendence. The New Atheists (such as Christopher Hitchens, Richard Dawkins, Sam Harris, and Daniel Dennett) are particularly adamant in their rejection of God, the supremacy of science, and the evil of religious belief.

At the same time, the fact/faith distinction allows some de facto secular naturalists to think of themselves as theists by removing God to the realm of faith rather than fact and by rejecting any involvement of God in the material world. Thus, for example, many hold to a purely naturalistic version of evolution (i.e. a system of evolution that denies any design or divine involvement in the process) while at the same time claiming belief in God. This is more of a deistic god—a God who cannot and does not intervene in the world—than the God of biblical theism.

Question 1: Where Did I Come From?

Human beings are the result of impersonal chemical processes and random mutations in the genetic code of earlier forms of life going back to single celled organisms.

No one is really sure how or why the universe came into existence or even if it eternal, though the best indication is that our current universe was the result of a unique event (a *"singularity"*) which we call the Big Bang. At this point matter and energy came into existence, and with them, space, time, and the laws of physics. Aside from matter and energy, nothing exists. Eventually, by the laws of physics, matter came together to form galaxies, nebulae, stars, and planets. On earth, the environment included the chemicals and the energy (probably through lightning) to produce organic chemicals in what we call the primordial soup. The organic compounds in the soup eventually somehow came to life, producing the first living cells. These living cells eventually developed or acquired DNA.

With DNA, the cells were able to pass the instructions for copying the organism down to their descendants. Since DNA sometimes does not produce identical copies—a process known as mutation—the living organisms were not all identical to each other.

Those with favorable traits tended to survive and pass those traits down to their offspring, and eventually enough mutations accumulated so that new species developed. Complexity was beneficial for survival, and so more complex organisms developed, starting with multi-celled creatures. This process accounts for the development of all of the different life forms on the planet, from amoebas to redwoods, molds to whales, house flies to humanity.

In essence, we are no different from any other creature, no worse and certainly no better. Humanity has no unique place or purpose in the universe different from any other creature. There is no overarching purpose or meaning to life, and at our death we become an inert mass of chemicals. We act as if there is meaning; we search for it or invent it, presumably because this gave our species some survival advantage despite being based on false perceptions about the world. Similarly, we act as if good and evil exist—in fact, we make moral judgments regularly—despite the fact that good and evil are also false ideas about the nature of reality. Morality does have survival value, however, and so humans with a sense of right and wrong tended to survive and pass the morality gene down. From an evolutionary perspective, the only right and wrong would have to do with whether or not you pass your genes down to the next generation. Secular naturalists tend not to emphasize this point, instead arguing that morality is situational and relative.

In some ways, however, the discussion of purpose, meaning, and morality is a red herring. These ideas are products of our consciousness, but our consciousness is itself a result of electro-chemical reactions in our brain. Given that chemical reactions are involuntary, there is very little room for free will, creative or original thought, or any other type of voluntary action at all. Once again, however, we have the illusion of free will because it gives us a survival advantage despite being contrary to the nature of reality. This leaves secular naturalists who debate theists in an awkward position: they must make their case and urge you to accept their argument. But to do that, you must have free will, which they deny exists.

Question 2: What is Wrong with the World?

The problems that human beings face are a result of genetics, or societal forces beyond their control, or both.

In a purely naturalistic context, the issue of "sin" or "evil" is nonsensical: if the physical world of matter and energy are all that exists, then "whatever is, is right," as Alexander Pope put it. Good and evil cannot exist as such, because they are neither matter nor energy. They are simply creations of our mind which proved useful for the survival of the species.

That said, pain and suffering are part of the human experience. Like everything else about us, suffering comes from three sources: our genes, our environment, and/or society. Genetics is frequently cited as a source for personal problems. There is a constant search for the gene(s) responsible for everything from birth defects to high cholesterol to obesity to addictions. This absolves the individual for personal responsibility in any of the areas that have a genetic basis, even if, for example, lifestyle changes would eliminate the problem.

A second source of pain and suffering is disruptions in the natural world, such as floods, droughts, tsunamis, earthquakes, volcanic eruptions, or asteroid strikes. Although such things have happened throughout time, human activity is increasingly blamed for these catastrophes, whether because of overpopulation or emissions of excessive amounts of greenhouse gases. Since these can no longer be described as "acts of God," someone or something has to take the blame so that we are not left completely at the mercy of forces beyond our control. In other words, we need to act as our own (and as the planet's) savior because the alternative—being helpless before a great, impersonal, and possibly malevolent universe—is psychologically intolerable.[1]

This brings us to the third and most important source of pain and suffering: society itself. Different thinkers identify different combinations of societal forces that create our problems, but these forces generally fall into three broad categories. The first is traditional ideas of morality and especially sexuality. These moral norms repress our sexual desires, and this repression has been seen as a source of psychological problems since Sigmund Freud. Traditional morality causes unnecessary feelings of guilt about our sexual impulses and results in judgmental behavior and arbitrary laws on marriage. In addition to restricting personal behavior, moral norms derived from Christianity also put constraints on what science and technology are permitted to do (for example, by opposition to destroying embryos for stem cells, or to cloning humans); these norms also value people who cannot contribute to society and who use scarce resources that could better be spent elsewhere (for example, the disabled, the unborn, the old and infirm).

A second problem area in society for some secular naturalists is our political and economic system,

---

[1] Human responsibility for environmental problems is the central feature of the Gaian worldview discussed in chapter 7.

though the argument here could go in two different directions. For liberals, the problem is capitalism and the military-industrial complex, which together produce greenhouse gases and other pollution, encourage greed, discourage sustainability, and lead us into wars to take the resources that we "need" to fulfill our wants. For conservatives, the problem is creeping socialism that takes away initiative and responsibility, promotes dependency on government, and destroys personal liberty.

The third problem area in society is religion. In addition to its role in supporting traditional moral ideas, religion poisons the well in several other ways. For example, religion accepts something other than science as a source of truth and thus is by definition irrational by the premises of scientism. If the religious belief claims any kind of objective truth in any area, or if it believes that God can and does act in this world, it violates the fact/faith distinction. This would be a major problem for the secular naturalist, since losing the fact/faith distinction otherwise would violate the fundamental premise that everything in the universe is made up of matter and energy and can be explained via the laws of science.

Along with these theoretical problems, religious belief also creates moral problems. Monotheistic religions in particular are by their nature intolerant and dogmatic, insisting on the superiority of their beliefs over all other belief systems and demanding that others follow them. This leads to hatred and bigotry against non-believers and therefore to terrorism and violence.

In all these cases, personal responsibility for pain and suffering is discounted. The only responsibility human beings have is through their roles in society. But even there, the emphasis is on institutions and structures, not so much the people themselves (except for religious and/or political leaders who hold views counter to the secular naturalist). We are either cogs in a machine or are so conditioned by society that we are not responsible ultimately for our own attitudes and ignorance.

Question 3: Is There a Solution?

The solution is to work toward a worldly utopia based on an ideological system that solves the key problem(s) facing society.

Secular naturalism's great hope is the creation of a worldly utopia where all peoples will live long, fulfilled lives, with all their needs met, in peace and harmony with each other. This involves solving the two key problems of genetics and society. In terms of genetics, it is already possible to screen for various genetic conditions and even for the propensity to develop some diseases. As this testing improves, we will be able to produce children who will not have to deal with serious genetic challenges. Further research into longevity and biotechnologies will extend people's lives and will give them capabilities no human has today. So we will harness science and technology to improve the species and take control of our own evolution.

For these technologies to be developed and deployed, and for any of the utopian visions to take hold, society will need to change. This is where specific ideological solutions move to center stage. Freud, for example, argued that human unhappiness was caused by repressing the sex drive. Although Freud thought that this could be repaired through psychoanalysis, the leaders of the sexual revolution of the 1960s and '70s thought of a more direct route to solve the problem: by getting rid of traditional morality and allowing for free expression of our sexual appetites, we will decrease mental illness and produce happier, better-adjusted people. To undermine traditional moral notions so that we can be sexually liberated, curricula must be introduced into the schools to re-educate children away from their parents' values toward sexual freedom, openness to homosexuality, and so on. Although the sexual revolution has had the opposite effect from the one predicted, causing more pain and suffering and no real liberation, this thinking continues to influence the culture.

Alternately, the problem could be economic injustice rooted in the inequalities that are central to capitalism, as Marxism, communism, and socialism have argued. The solution then is to redistribute income by taking it from those who are most successful at making it, and giving it to those who are less successful. Similarly, health care and other necessities need more equitable distribution, so these will need to move out of the private sector and into the control of the state.

On the "conservative" side, the solution could be a free-wheeling capitalism devoid of moral restraint, a kind of "survival of the fittest" applied to economics that rewards those who out-compete their rivals, however ethically shady their actions might be. This will ultimately produce the best technologies, the best and most abundant goods, and the most overall prosperity of any economic system yet devised. By achieving economic prosperity, we can fund medical research and solve the world's problems using the ever-efficient free market.

More simply, the problem may be religion. By dividing people, religion is seen as a source of conflict and hatred in the world, as well as introducing a values system that prevents the free development of science and technology by muddying the waters with moral issues. The solution is either to eliminate religion entirely, or to silence its voice in public policy discussions to prevent it from "imposing" its views on society. The essence of *secularism* is the idea that religious beliefs, if they are held at all, are to be personal and must not play any role in public life or political discussion. Thus, for example, religious symbols on public land are to be removed, all reference to religion must be expunged from government buildings and monuments, the religious dimensions of Western history are to be ignored or denied, etc. In short, religion is to be marginalized and religious views are to be systematically excluded from public life.

The common thread through all these solutions is the necessity of re-educating youth in a new value structure to create the conditions for the future utopia. Although it promises personal fulfillment and freedom from want, however, like all utopian systems this one will inevitably become totalitarian, since resistance to its program will prevent the arrival of the promised humanistic golden age. This is why militant secularism is needed: religious views threaten to derail or at least delay the triumph of the ideology and the better world that will result from it.

Question 4: What is My Purpose?

Life's purpose is self-fulfillment, whatever that means to each individual.

Since life has no objective meaning or purpose, we have to decide for ourselves what gives us satisfaction and pursue that.

Following Freud, sexual self-expression is seen as a fundamental element of self-fulfillment in modern secular culture, as evidenced by the explosive growth of the pornography industry, by the push in some areas to legalize prostitution, by the growing prominence of homosexuality and the push for same sex marriage, and by the content of advertising, popular music, and media. Along with sex, money (and the time, material possessions and comforts it can buy) is another frequent goal in life, though studies show that once basic needs are met, increasing income does not result in increasing happiness. Power and influence, respect, fame, all are elements that many people see as important for self-fulfillment.

More sophisticated thinkers in secular culture realize that these material benefits cannot give us a true sense of purpose or satisfaction with life. Probably the best known attempt to explain this comes from psychologist Abraham Maslow. Maslow posited that we have a number of fundamental needs which must be met. Once we meet these, we move on to more sophisticated desires, then still more sophisticated desires, until finally we reach the level of self-actualization. The self-actualized person is tolerant, open-minded, spontaneous, benevolent, moral—in other words, all the character traits admired by Maslow. The solution to the problem of suffering, then, is to create institutional structures and educational systems that will provide for people's basic needs (physical needs, safety, love, and self-esteem) so they can be encouraged to move on to self-actualization.

Unfortunately, however, if self-fulfillment is a route to giving life meaning and purpose, it is ultimately a lie. As atheist philosopher Bertrand Russell observed, "Unless you assume a God, the question of life's purpose is meaningless." In a world of matter and energy, life has no purpose because the universe is devoid of meaning, an idea known as *nihilism*. Although there have been many attempts to escape the trap of nihilism, it is the inevitable, logical conclusion of the premises of secular naturalism, scientism, and the fact/faith distinction. This is why life's purpose is reduced to personal satisfaction: any higher goal would be purely arbitrary since meaning, value, significance, and purpose are all matters of faith, not fact.

3—Postmodernism

Postmodernism is extraordinarily difficult—some would say impossible—to define. In broad terms, it is a reaction against modernity and the Enlightenment tradition, and thus against important elements of secular naturalism. At the same time, some analysts see it as a subset of secular naturalism and argue that postmodernism does not exist at all, but is simply a more extreme form of modern thought. Others see postmodernism as less a system of thought than an attitude.

Postmodernism is built on the premises that absolute truth does not exist, that objectivity is impossible, and that everything we think of as true is a product of culture (a *social construct*, to use the language of postmodernism). This has several implications:

- Truth is personal: something can be true for one person but not for another.
- Truth is also political: social power defines reality, and thus reality can change as society does.
- Language is particularly important both as a social construct and as the means by which society can either preserve the status quo or change into new realities. As a result, language is highly politicized in postmodernism, with control of words seen as essential to create a better world.

41

- Hard binary categories, such as male and female, heterosexual and homosexual, or black and white, are especially pernicious social constructs. These are better viewed as places on a continuum, with no clear, hard and fast definitions or distinctions between the apparent polarities. A more complete view of life would recognize these multiple realities rather than reduce them to a single reality dictated to us by our culture.

- Since truth is relative, no culture can claim to be superior to any other. Postmoderns reject the idea of a *metanarrative* (i.e. an overarching story explaining history or its trajectory), and so it is thus wrong to think of Western Civilization as better than non-Western cultures, and modernity, capitalism, or any other systems as the wave of the future globally.

These ideas are a direct challenge to all truth claims, whether those of religion or scientism.[2]

Despite the differences in concepts of truth, postmoderns often share many of the answers to the fundamental worldview questions with secular naturalists. In their rejection of scientism, however, they are often more open to various paths to spirituality drawn from New Age ideas, particularly goddess worship (because of their opposition to sexism) and eco-spirituality (see chapter 7). Their understanding of "truth," makes postmoderns systematically open to incorporating ideas drawn from a variety of other worldviews since their acceptance of an idea makes it "true for them."

---

[2] See the introduction to the chapter on Secular Naturalism for an explanation of scientism.

Given the diversity of postmodernism, it is very difficult to give definitive answers from this perspective to the different worldview questions. In particular, it is important to distinguish between people who have adopted some of the ideas and terminology of postmodernism without actually thinking it through (sometimes called "*amateur postmoderns*"), and those who understand postmodernism and have accepted its view of the world ("*professional postmoderns*"). The following are common answers to the worldview questions among "professional postmoderns" in America. Once again, however, it is important to recognize that more than any other worldview, the answers may vary wildly from one postmodern to another. As always, do not assume you know what people think or believe; ask for specifics and explanations.

Question 1: Where Did I Come From?

Human beings are the result of impersonal chemical processes and random mutations in the genetic code of earlier forms of life going back to single celled organisms.

Most postmoderns accept the secular naturalist understanding of origins.

Question 2: What is Wrong with the World?

The problems that human beings face are a result of institutionalized oppression.

Although they do not typically speak in these terms, postmoderns tend to view the world as a zero sum game, that is, if one person advances, it must be at the expense of another. In particular, any group that

44

gains power must do so by taking it away from another—in other words, differences in power are caused by oppression. As a result, postmodernists tend to be particularly critical of capitalism, which in their view is based on unhealthy competition rather than cooperation, produces winners and losers, and thus is intrinsically oppressive since the winners could only win by exploiting the losers. To put it differently, the poor are poor because the rich are rich.

Along with capitalism, Western liberal democracy is also founded on a system of institutionalized power and oppression that has allowed elites (typically defined as rich white heterosexual males) to monopolize power. As a result of the competitive ideology that the political system shares with capitalism, Western culture promotes the wealthy over the poor, whites over blacks, men over women, heterosexual over homosexual. This leads to the oppression of the poor, people of color, homosexual, bisexual, and transgendered individuals, and women.

To take this one step further, since western culture dominates the globe, it must have achieved this through oppressing and exploiting other cultures.

At this point the cultural relativity of the postmodernist begins to break down. Although in principle they believe that no culture is superior to any other, in practice they tend to blame Western society for all the wrongs in the world and extol the virtues of non-Western cultures. The zero sum game is at work here as well: because oppression is wrong, the oppressor loses virtue, which passes to the oppressed. So Western civilization is evil and non-Western cultures are good.

Similarly, oppressed groups (women, ethnic and racial minorities, the poor, homosexuals, the transgendered, etc.) are seen as having moral authority that those in power lack. This is why feminists, for example, support homosexual rights which would seem to have no connection to their basic cause, and why both of them often offer support to various Muslim groups even though those groups may oppose women's rights and homosexuality: they are all "oppressed" groups by the institutional power structures of the West, and therefore they are all in some sense virtuous and therefore on the same side in the fight against oppression.

Question 3: Is There a Solution?

The solution is to work toward a worldly utopia based on unrestricted personal freedom enforced by government regulation.

Since the fundamental problem in society is that the elites monopolize power and use it to exploit the weak, the solution is to get political power to ensure that the oppressed are given their rights. This means an end to imposing the elite's vision of reality on society, but instead giving each person the freedom to define reality for her or himself.

Ironically, given their rejection of binary categories, postmoderns tend to support identity politics as a way of creating grievance groups that can pressure society to change. Although the traditional categories of race, class, and gender continue to be important, the cutting edge of this movement is in the area of sexuality, which has increasingly become the central issue in discussions of freedom and personal identity.

In the wake of the sexual revolution, the postmodern rejection of rigid categories has led to the idea of *sexual orientation* or *sexual identity*, based on the idea that everyone's sexuality falls on a continuum between heterosexuality and homosexuality. This sexual orientation is immutable: you are born with your orientation and it cannot change. No particular orientation on the continuum is superior to any other.

Gender identity follows from there. The concept of gender identity is built on the same postmodern rejection of rigid categories: it argues that gender is not biologically determined nor is it as simple as male or female. Instead, we are all on a continuum from masculine to feminine. Unlike your sexual orientation, however, gender is a matter of choice: whatever our biological characteristics, we have the right to determine whether we want to be male or female on any particular day. So sexual orientation is biologically determined and unchangeable, but gender is not.

Society has historically sought to impose its rigid, binary categories of male and female on sexual minorities for centuries. The next stage of human liberation is thus to free these sexual minorities from the oppressive structures of society by legally enforcing people's right to define their own gender, and by extending traditional heterosexual benefits and status—including marriage—to those with other sexual orientations.

Of course, conferring legal benefits only solves part of the problem. People need to be free from social stigma as well. This is to be accomplished in two ways. First, educators shaped by postmodernism indoctrinate children from a young age with these ideas of sexual orientation and gender identity (including encouraging sexual experimentation and exploration of different orientations); this integrates well with the kinds of sexual education promoted by many versions of secular naturalism.

Second, postmodernists rely on legislation to enforce their vision of society. Language is a particularly potent tool for controlling culture since it shapes how we think. One of the first goals is therefore to gain control of language through speech codes and criminalizing certain kinds of statements as "hate crimes." In particular, this means attacking anyone who claims to know objective truth as intolerant, hateful, and bigoted. Along with eliminating free speech in the name of "tolerance" and the individual's "right not to be offended," the postmodernist pushes for laws against "oppression" of marginalized groups. The postmodernist looks to the courts or legislatures to force changes in society designed to undermine the power of rich white heterosexual men. In this way they hope to create a utopia where individual choice is the only norm, and where no one or nothing can question a person's freedom to define her- or himself any way he or she chooses. In the process, of course, they set up a new set of elites dedicated to taking power away from the old elites.

Since the ideological postmodernist sees Western society and especially capitalism as the ultimate sources of oppression, it is not surprising that those who advocate the solution described here also frequently tend to join in a variety of other left wing causes, including anti-colonialism and opposition to US military intervention abroad; anti-militarism and shifting of budget priorities away from the military to social programs at home; an expanded social safety net; universal health care; anti-capitalism and socialism; anti-corporate, pro-government policies; radical environmentalism; etc. In general, they favor increased government involvement in all areas of life except in areas of sexual morality. The assumption is that the state will do better at taking care of people—especially those currently without power—than the free market does.

Question 4: What is My Purpose?

Life's purpose is to create a world where each individual is free to live out her or his own self-defined identity, free of judgment from others, with all essential needs guaranteed to be supplied by society.

As we have seen, freedom and identity in postmodernism are closely tied to sexuality, though race and class are also important components. Personal freedom is one of the key goals of the movement, in practice defined as the ability to pursue any form of sexuality and sexual and gender identity you choose.

This insistence on the individual's right to define her- or himself any way s/he chooses ties in with postmodernism's violent reaction against anyone making absolute truth claims, particularly in matters of ethics, morality, or lifestyle choices: absolutes are limits on your freedom to define yourself. To make any kind of negative ethical judgment on another's lifestyle is to be intolerant or bigoted. And the government ought to legislate against this kind of bigotry through outlawing expression of these views via speech codes and hate crimes legislation.

Aside from sexual freedom, the ideological postmodernist paradoxically tends to see the increased governmental control and regulation to be the solution to the rest of the problems of society. Since free enterprise and the private sector produce inequality, the public sector must act to eliminate it. And the postmodernist is willing to sacrifice most traditional ideas of freedom in return for security and freedom from criticism for their lifestyles. Cradle to grave universal health care (including contraception and abortion to allow for sexual freedom), food, federally subsidized mortgages, funding for college and forgiveness of college loans, all should be guaranteed regardless of ability to pay. Government regulation should restrict the growth of the wealth of corporations and individuals and should set and enforce strict environmental rules regardless of the impact on the economy. In this way, we can create a utopian world where everyone's needs are met and their sexual freedom and identity preserved and affirmed.

Postmodernism's promise, particularly with regard to sexual liberation, has not had positive results in real life. The pursuit of sexual self-expression has led to a tremendous growth in out-of-wedlock births and single parent households—the single greatest predictor of poverty and of a wide range of other social ills—as well as to an epidemic of STDs, depression (particularly among sexually active women), and the high rate of abortion (about 1/3 of what would have been the current generation of college students has been aborted).

Further, at root, postmodernism's fundamental premises are so flawed as to be incoherent: absolute truth absolutely does not exist; objectivity is objectively impossible; it is universally true that all "truths" are social constructs; it is universally and objectively true that truth is personal and subjective. It is no wonder, then, that postmodernism is declining everywhere except in universities. And even there, the coursework relies on books written 20-30 years ago. It is unclear what will replace it.

Yet although postmodernism is on its way out as a system of thought, it continues as an attitude toward truth, "tolerance," and culture, particularly among "amateur postmoderns." We see this in a wide range of areas, but to consider just one, we will look at its impact on religious ideas in America.

Postscript: Postmodern Religion

Although there are a variety of religious views espoused by postmodernists, including eco-spirituality (see chapter 7), the most common religion among "amateur postmoderns" is *Moralistic Therapeutic Deism*. First analyzed by Christian Smith and Melinda Lundquist Denton, Moralistic Therapeutic Deism is not a fully defined worldview. Rather, it is a widely held set of religious beliefs, particularly among younger people from a wide range of religions, as well as among those who do not see themselves as part of a formal religion and those who describe themselves as "spiritual, not religious."

Moralistic Therapeutic Deism is built around five ideas:

1. A god exists who created and ordered the world and watches over human life on earth.
2. God wants people to be good, nice, and fair to each other, as taught in the Bible and by most world religions.
3. The central goal of life is to be happy and to feel good about oneself.
4. God is not particularly involved in one's life except when needed to solve a problem.
5. Good people go to heaven when they die.

These religious beliefs are *moralistic* because of points 2 and 3 above, and *therapeutic* because of points

3 and 4. Historically, *deism* saw god as simply a creator who was uninvolved with the universe. Smith and Denton see a therapeutic form of deism in this system because god is largely uninvolved with the creation, makes no demands, and only acts to help solve problems for us (points 1 and 4).

Moralistic Therapeutic Deism is an almost ideal amateur postmodern religion. It is non-dogmatic, so you are free to believe and follow whatever religion you like; it is inclusive, offering acceptance to anyone who is a nice person; it is tolerant, since it rejects the idea of judging anyone else's beliefs or practices. In short, it embodies the cardinal virtues of amateur postmodernism.

Of course, Moralistic Therapeutic Deism also cuts itself off from the historic traditions of the world's great religions and never deals with the logical contradictions inherent in the competing truth claims of these religions. Since there is no objective truth, these contradictions aren't a problem—everything is personal perspective. In terms of Christianity, Moralistic Therapeutic Deism specifically rejects the idea of the Fall and original sin, as well as the uniqueness of the redemption offered by Christ.

At the same time, however, the Moralistic Therapeutic Deist makes truth claims that go well beyond the personal. They believe that at their core, all religions are essentially the same (point 2) and lead to the same destination (point 5). They frequently describe this as many paths that lead to the top of the same mountain. Yet the different religions do not see themselves this way. Who is to say that Moralistic Therapeutic Deism is more objectively true than they are? Who gave the Moralistic Therapeutic Deist a spiritual helicopter to fly up the mountain to see that everyone is heading for the same destination? How do they know that all religions end up there? Why aren't the Moralistic Therapeutic Deists as bound by social constructs as those who hold to traditional religions? While other issues could be raised, these illustrate that the kinds of logical problems that arise in connection with postmodernism apply as well to Moralistic Therapeutic Deism.

In His name

4—Islam

Islam is one of the largest religions in the world, second only to Christianity, and is one of the fastest growing. There are two main branches in Islam: *Sunni*, or "orthodox" Islam, and *Shi'a*, the dominant version of Islam in Iran and Iraq; the third largest group is the *Sufi*, a form of Muslim mysticism. There are a number of sub-groups as well, the most important being the ultra-conservative *Wahhabi*. *Wahhabism* is a branch of *Sunni* Islam and the state religion of Saudi Arabia, which funds many mosques and Muslim schools around the world.

Truth in Islam is found in the Quran, which is believed to be the very words of God, called Allah in Arabic. Muslims have traditionally argued that it cannot be translated out of Arabic since no translation can completely convey the full meaning of the text: all "translations" are therefore really commentaries. Because the Quran is the word of Allah, it is to be believed literally, which is why there is limited theological discussion (as opposed to legal interpretation) within Islam.

Because of the emphasis on literal reading of the Quran, there has always been a certain amount of tension about how to deal with ideas coming from foreign cultures. The general trend has been to incorporate practical learning, while rejecting speculative or theoretical ideas. This enabled the Muslim world to excel during its Golden Age in

53

technology, mathematics, astronomy, geography, and to some extent medicine, though without developing theoretical explanations of why the world works the way it does.

For example, a number of prominent medieval Muslim scholars attacked the emerging idea of scientific law: since the Quran teaches that Allah directly controls everything that happens, any suggestion that there were laws of nature was dismissed as an attempt to limit Allah's freedom. At the same time, in some places various forms of folk Islam have developed that combine Islam with indigenous religions to produce belief systems wildly at odds with basic Muslim ideas.

About 10% of the approximately one billion Muslims around the world are Islamists, that is, people dedicated to bringing the whole world under *sharia* (Quranic law). A subset of these advocate *jihad* as the means to accomplish this. The other 90% of Muslims tend to be less committed to this goal, though recent surveys indicate that the majority of Muslims in Britain want to see *sharia* implemented there, and many see suicide bombing against civilian targets as legitimate. The reason is simple: Mohammed was a warlord and the teachings of the Quran as outlined below can support these kinds of ideas and attitudes. Most Muslims do not actually live consistently with the dictates of their religion any more than Christians do, though to understand the Muslim worldview, it is important to go back to the Quran for the answers to the fundamental worldview questions.

Question 1: Where Did I Come From?

Human beings are created by Allah, though they are not made in His image.

Allah created all things and directly controls everything that happens in the universe. In addition to the physical world, Allah also created angels—intelligent spiritual beings without free will who carry out Allah's instructions—and the *jinn*, intelligent creatures made out of smokeless fire who have free will and who are inherently mischievous (though not overly intelligent). Allah consulted with the angels about who would be his vice-regent (*Caliph*) on earth and decided upon man, whom Allah had created and endowed with intelligence and free will. The angels and Iblis, one of the *jinn*, tried to talk Allah out of this because of man's potential for violence and mischief, but Allah rejected their advice on the grounds that He knew more than they did about human potential. (We will return to Iblis when we discuss what is wrong with the world.)

Allah created Adam as the first soul from a blob of mud—the Quran uses a word that means an unclean liquid or a chewed up object like cud—and then created Eve from him as the second soul. From these two descend all of humanity. They are not, however, made in the image of Allah. Nothing and no one can be the image of Allah because any image would contradict His greatness and transcendence. To suggest that anything can be an image of Allah is at best evidence of ignorance and at worst is blasphemous. Rather than the image of Allah, human dignity comes from our obedience to Allah as his vice-regents in this world—in other words it depends on how well we obey Allah, not on anything in our nature. Unbelievers therefore have less dignity and worth than the faithful.

The fact that we are all descended from Adam and Eve means that the family (husband, wife, and legal

56

children) is the fundamental unit of society as established by Allah. Men and women have complementary but essential roles, and all peoples are members of one extended family. Islam thus teaches that we should thus regard each other as siblings and not divide ourselves on the basis of race, skin color, or nationality.

However, this does not mean that in Islam all people are equal. In Islamic law, a woman's testimony is worth half a man's, and the Quran states that women are much less likely to enter Heaven than men. And since human rights and human dignity are ultimately a matter of Allah's will and are based on submitting to his authority, those who refuse to convert to Islam but desire to live in a Muslim-ruled society forfeit their rights except as granted by the Muslim authorities in a "concessionary charter" (*dhimma*). We will discuss this further under Question 4.

Further, just as Christians have not always acted consistently with their beliefs, the anti-racist concepts within Islam often break down, particularly in the face of tribalism in the Middle East as demonstrated by the tensions between Arab *Sunni* and the Kurdish *Sunni* in Iraq, as well as between Arabs, Iranians, Turks, and other ethnic groups.

Question 2: What is Wrong with the World?

Sin and suffering exist by Allah's will and the free will of *jinn* and humans who refuse to submit to the will of Allah, either because they are deceived or because of the self. There is no original sin.

Sin and suffering entered the world because of Iblis. Allah commanded the angels and the *jinn* to bow down to Adam and Eve. The angels did so—they have no free will—but Iblis refused because he thought it was beneath his dignity: he was made of fire, a ᴸ. substance than the mud from which Adam was maᵤ. Allah then decreed that Iblis would be punished for his refusal at the end of time; Iblis responded that if he has until then, he would lead as many of Adam's descendants astray as he could to show just how poor a choice humanity was to be Allah's vice-regent. Allah accepted this, but promised hellfire as Iblis's recompense.

Iblis, now titled *Shaitan* (the Devil or the Evil One), led Adam and Eve astray, and now is permitted by Allah to roam the earth, testing humans and *jinn* to see if he can corrupt them through temptation and false ideas. Iblis/*Shaitan* is thus not Allah's enemy—he is simply a creature performing a task in accordance with the will of Allah. But he is most certainly humanity's enemy.

All people are born Muslims because they are born in a state of innocence without original sin, just like Adam and Eve were. As they grow, however, they are led away from Islam by lies and temptations introduced originally by *Shaitan*, but now taught by their parents, by false religions, by societies that have not yet submitted to the will of Allah, by *jinn*, and by *Shaitan* himself. In the Quran, it even states that Allah guides some and misguides others, with the result that those who are guided follow Allah, and those who are misguided turn away from him (Sura 14:4). This is in keeping with Allah's title as "the Deceiver," one of the Ninety-Nine Names of Allah in Islam, as well as with the idea that Allah can do whatever He wills without reason or explanation.

Along with the Devil and his lies, *nafs* (the self, the ego, or the psyche) is also a source of evil. From the self come seven great sins: pride, greed, jealousy, lust,

back-biting, stinginess, and malice. The self is so full of sin and so difficult to deal with that Mohammed himself identified *jihad* against enemies of Islam as a lesser or easier *jihad* than the *jihad* against the self. How *nafs* became so corrupt is never explained, given that infants are born in a state of innocence. Although Islam rejects original sin, it comes very close to the concept with this understanding of *nafs* as a major source of evil in all of our lives.

Question 3: What is the Solution?

The solution to the world's problems is for people to submit to the will of Allah and become faithful Muslims. Even this is no guarantee of final salvation, however.

The core of Islam is found in the Five Pillars: *Shahadah*, the creed, "there is no God but Allah and Mohammed is His prophet;" *Salah*, liturgical prayers in Arabic five times per day, facing Mecca; *Zakah*, alms giving; *Sawm*, ritual fasting during the holy month of Ramadan; and *Hajj*, pilgrimage to Mecca once in your lifetime if possible. *Shi'a* Islam adds *Jihad* as a sixth pillar.

Islam is primarily a religion of orthopraxy—right practice—rather than orthodoxy—right doctrine. Divisions within Islam rarely deal with doctrine; rather, they focus on what it means to live as a Muslim. Thus Islam does not have theologians so much as *ulema* or *mullahs*, that is, experts in *sharia* (Islamic law).

Beyond the Five Pillars, each separate sect within Islam has its own rituals and rites that its adherents must perform and that they consider true Islam. From a strict perspective, all others sects are therefore by definition apostate because they are not following the proper practices that a true Muslim must

do. Switching sects is also considered apostasy. The rejection of alternate forms of Islam extends beyond the obvious divisions of *Sunni*, *Shi'a*, and *Sufi* to the smaller sects and sub-groups in these larger divisions. This helps account for the Muslim-on-Muslim violence in places like Iraq and Afghanistan.

Even following correct practice does not guarantee entrance into Paradise, however. Ultimately, one's fate is determined entirely by the will of Allah. Upon death, we will all pass across the Bridge of Judgment. Unbelievers fall off the bridge into Hell; believers will be met by Mohammed, who will guide those Allah accepts to safety, while the rest will fall into Hell as well. Unfaithful Muslims will spend some time in Hell to purge them from their sins, after which Allah will lift them out and bring them into Paradise. According to Mohammed, most of the people in Hell are women, though Allah will permit some into Heaven.

Martyrs are guaranteed entrance into Paradise, however. According to Abu Huraira, a companion of Mohammed, Allah will accept five classes of people as martyrs: those who die of plague, abdominal disease, drowning, a falling building, and in fighting for Allah's cause (*Sahih Bukhari Hadith*, vol. 4, book 52, no. 82). Since the first four of these are acts of Allah, the only thing a person can do to guarantee entry into Heaven is to die while fighting in a *jihad*. The concept of martyrdom is thus very different from in Christianity: Christian martyrs are those put to death for their faith; Muslim martyrs are those who die fighting for Islam.

Heaven is described in hedonistic terms. There are seven gates to Heaven, and the higher the gate you are permitted to enter, the greater the pleasures available to you. The lowest gate gives you two "dark

60

eyed virgins." These are *houri*, beautiful women who are miraculously restored to virginity after use. The seventh gate gives you 72 virgins. Muslims are not permitted wine on earth, but they can have it in heaven. Banquets, beautiful palaces, and everything you desire is available for you, along with the company of friends and loved ones.

Question 4: What is My Purpose?

Our purpose is to submit to the will of Allah and to work to bring about *umma muslima*, a world in complete submission to Allah.

The Quran says that Allah created the *jinn* and humanity to worship Him (51:56-58). This worship must be done in the right ways, however, as revealed in the Quran. As a religion of orthopraxy, right actions are critical, and thus proper worship means submitting to the will of Allah—in fact, the word "Islam" means "submission" (not "peace," contrary to what some contemporary Muslims claim). As we have seen, however, each group claims to have the "true" Islam, leading to tensions and sometimes violence between the different sects. *umma - community*

In addition to personal submission to Allah, Muslims are part of a community, or *umma*. Ultimately, the entire world will eventually be part of the community of submission (*umma muslima*). Islam can spread in two ways. The first is *dawah*, "inviting" people to become Muslims. This is done through discussion and action, and is something all Muslims should engage in. (*Dawah* can also include efforts to strengthen the *umma* through inviting people to more faithful observance of Islam.) Though Muslims rarely talk about (or even admit having) evangelistic efforts in the U.S., there are a number of groups that are very active in *dawah* and in training their followers to spread Islam.

When *dawah* fails, Muslims can resort to the sword to spread the *umma*, following the example of Mohammed. *Jihad* technically is war for the defense of the faith, and Muslim apologists will regularly deny that Mohammed and his early successors fought any offensive wars. Yet an examination of Mohammed's career reveals that he labeled anyone who refused the invitation to become Muslim as an enemy and thus as subject to *jihad*—which was then defined as a defensive war against people whose rejection of Mohammed's message marked them as a threat to Islam.

Mohammed's interactions with the Jews of Medina is a good example of this, as is his successors' conquest of the Persian Empire and a large portion of the Eastern Roman (Byzantine) Empire, as well as the invasion of Europe by Muslims in the century following Mohammed's death. There is thus ample precedent within the career of Mohammed and in early Muslim history for advancing Islam through both persuasion and *jihad*. This is the explicit goal of many Islamist groups today in fulfillment of Islam's vision of a world in submission to the will of Allah and the supremacy of Islam.

Conquest is not automatically the same as forced conversion, of course. The Quran states that there is "no compulsion in religion," which is frequently cited in support of the idea that Islam allows for freedom of conscience. At the same time, however, all non-Muslims were expelled from Arabia, and non-Muslims living in Islamic states were historically governed by a *dhimma*, a concessionary charter that grants non-Muslims limited rights and protections. *Dhimmi* had to pay a special tax (the *jizya*) so that they "feel themselves subdued" by Islam even if they were indigenous peoples recently conquered or are native inhabitants of the country. They were thus seen as clearly inferior citizens to Muslims, a status reinforced by the prohibitions of non-Muslims testifying against Muslims in a court of law, and of holding authority over Muslims in any context.

Religious freedom was also severely restricted, a condition that continues to exist in many Muslim countries to this day. *Dhimmi* could not build new houses of worship, pray or read their scriptures aloud even at home, or have any form of public religious display, lest they offend Muslims. Sometimes, they were even required to offer their sons to be raised as Muslim slave-soldiers. Under these conditions, *dhimmi* were permitted to live within the *umma muslima*, though many people in conquered territories historically have converted to Islam to escape these exactions. Muslims do not consider these forced conversions, however, though by Western standards they were certainly coerced.

5—Eastern Religions

Eastern religions have had a significant cultural impact in the Western world over the past several decades. Different forms of Buddhism, Hinduism, and Taoism in particular have influenced American popular culture, whether through the Zen Buddhism of the Beatniks, Hinduism with the Beatles, Vedic medicine and yoga, Taoism through martial arts and health practices, or Tibetan Buddhism through the Tibetan Book of the Dead and the Dalai Lama. Although most popular forms of these religious ideas have been mixed generously with pagan ideas and Western science to form the New Age movement (see the next chapter), in their original form they continue to exert an important influence on Western culture. In this chapter, we will look at the Eastern religions themselves and identify some of the key worldview ideas that underpin them.

This is not an easy task. Although there are common themes, each religion answers the four basic worldview questions in somewhat different ways. The dharmic religions (Hinduism, Buddhism, Jainism, Sikhism) have a different philosophical approach than the East Asian religions (Confucianism, Taoism, Shintoism), coming from differences in their underlying worldviews. Even within a single religious tradition, there can be a tremendous diversity: there are monistic, dualistic, pantheistic, polytheistic, monotheistic, and atheistic approaches to Hinduism, and Buddhism is nearly as complex, to take just two examples.

At the same time, most of these philosophies and religions do share a number of common elements, the most important of which is a particular approach to metaphysics (the branch of philosophy dealing with the ultimate nature of reality). Eastern thought tends to be built around the assumption that the world (or at least the distinctions between things in the world) is an illusion, and that ultimately, all things are really one, an idea known as *monism*. In many systems, this underlying unity is identified with or includes god, and thus the systems are not only monistic, but pantheistic.

One consequence of Eastern monism is that the best use of your mind is to see beyond the illusion to the ultimate unity of all things. This is not a matter of rational activity. Reality is fundamentally non-rational and built upon ignorance and silence rather than knowledge. In most Eastern systems, truth is not found through reason at all, but through intuition and mystical experience. The goal is to silence our thoughts, not develop them. This is why, for all the monumental technological, engineering, and artistic achievements of Asia, they never developed experimental science. Philosophical speculation about the world was as far as they got, because ultimately the highest kind of knowledge was not knowledge of the physical world of illusion, but of the reality behind it. This kind of knowledge can only be achieved through meditation, ritual, or other activities, not through studying the world. It is thus very difficult to come up with a rational, systematic explanation of Eastern thought. The very different starting assumptions about the nature of reality make it extraordinarily difficult for people shaped by Western culture to grasp these religions.

It is also difficult to fit Eastern religions into the four worldview questions, though it can be done. The main difficulty is that questions 3 and 4 tend to overlap even more than in other worldviews, largely because of the particular way monism works out in Asian thought. The answers to the questions differ as well from religion to religion, though there is enough common ground between that some generalizations can be made about Eastern approaches to the worldview questions, with adjustments to the answers for each individual system.

Since the most influential Eastern religions in the West are Hinduism, Buddhism, and Taoism, we will focus on these three.

Question 1: Where Did I Come From?

Human beings exist as the result of karmic balance being passed forward from previous lifetimes.

In Eastern religions, ultimate reality is most often seen as impersonal, and personal existence is seen as an illusion that keeps us from achieving unity with that ultimate reality. Most Eastern religions accept the idea of karma, the cosmic law of cause and effect, and of reincarnation or rebirth. The law of karma says that actions done in one lifetime cause effects in the next. Your place in life today is a result of the actions you performed in a previous lifetime, and you are trapped in an endless and meaningless cycle of birth and rebirth until such time as you achieve enlightenment and break out of the cycle.

In *Hinduism*, people are incarnations of an eternal, individual soul (*atman*) that exists in relationship with the universal soul (*Brahman*). Depending on the school of Hinduism, *atman* may be a fragment of *Brahman*, it could be separate from *Brahman*, or it could contain the fullness of *Brahman* within itself. However it is understood, *atman* is embodied over successive incarnations as animals or humans, the details of the specific incarnation depending on the karma inherited from previous lifetimes. (This will be discussed further below.) There is thus no significant difference between human life and animal life, leading many devout Hindus (though not all) to become vegetarians. Each individual soul has lived innumerable lives at varying levels in the hierarchy of living creatures, though it retains no memory or other conscious connection with those previous lives. It continues to be reincarnated, however, because of its desire to enjoy the pleasures of physical life.

In *Buddhism*, individual existence is an illusion caused by desire, and the soul, if it exists at all, is an "afflictive misunderstanding" (more on this later). In fact, the entire world that we perceive is an illusion. All of what we think of as reality is in a constant state of flux, including human life. Since things that are constantly changing cannot be bedrock reality, the impermanence of the world demonstrates that it does not truly exist. Further, what we think of as the self is actually a collection of constantly changing physical and mental states, and so it too does not actually exist. In other words, what we think of as the "self" is actually the "non-self," the illusion of individual existence. If there is a reality underlying human life, it is the Buddha nature which sees through the illusion of separate existence and lives in a permanent state of bliss, experiencing the oneness of all things.

At the same time, there is a sense in which a form of the illusory self can continue after death, as the "mindstream" (as it is sometimes called) shaped by karma is passed forward. This is not reincarnation, since there is no soul that can be reincarnated, but a "rebirth," the karmic momentum of a previous life carrying forward into the next like a ripple on the ocean of being. This rebirth could be as an animal, a variety of supernatural beings, or a human depending on the nature of the karmic force.

In *Taoism*, the *tao* (the "way," that is, the order of the universe) is the origin of all things. From it spring the two principles of *yin* and *yang*, and the dynamic interaction of these two is the source of everything else. *Chi*, the breath of the Universe, is the source of life. Human beings are microcosms of the universe, with the five principle organs corresponding to the five elements, five directions, and five seasons of Chinese thought. Life lived according to the *tao* results in peace, love for all things, and long (perhaps immortal) life, though the truly enlightened person rejects concepts of individual identity in favor of seeing the unity of the *tao*. In early Taoism, you live just one lifetime and then dissolve back into the *tao*; in later Taoism, karma enters the picture, and with it, a vaguely defined concept of reincarnation. Your position in life today is a result of the karma you built up in previous lives.

Question 2: What is Wrong with the World?

Suffering is a result both of karma built up from wrong actions in previous lives, and of desire.

Suffering is caused by ignorance and by desire, which each contribute to our resistance to ultimate reality (however that is conceived) and tie us to the cycle of reincarnation or rebirth. All of our actions produce karma, a kind of moral cause and effect that shapes our next lifetime. Suffering is thus a result of negative karma produced by wrong actions done in a previous lifetime.

Evil per se does not exist in most versions of Eastern thought. In *Hinduism*, evil is variously described as failure to follow laws and rituals, the work of demons, buying into the illusory nature of the world, the outworking of karma, or the work of the gods themselves, who are thus the source of both good and evil. Evil is recognized as a proper part of the dynamic of the world, and is thus in a sense as good. In *Buddhism*, evil is failing to see that the world is an illusion, and that ultimate reality is found in the union of all things in permanent, unchanging bliss. In *Taoism*, everything that exists is the result of the *tao* (the order of the natural world) and can thus be described as good. What we call evil is the result of an imbalance between the forces of nature, which is itself part of the natural order and therefore part of a higher good.

Hinduism, Buddhism, and later Taoism all accept the idea of karma. In all cases, bad karma and suffering is a result of ignorance, which results in failing to live according to the *dharma* (the universal law in Hinduism, or the Buddha's teachings in Buddhism) or the *tao*. Not following the *dharma* or *tao* has consequences for both this life and future lives.

In *Hinduism, Buddhism* and *later versions of Taoism* that accept reincarnation, our status upon reincarnation or rebirth and our place in society as human beings depends entirely on our actions in the previous life, whether as an imprint on our *atman* (our eternal soul) or through creating a ripple in our mindstream. Even though we carry no memories of our previous lives with us, nonetheless the actions (and in some religious philosophies, the thoughts) we harbor in those lifetimes are causes which produce inevitable effects in our subsequent lives. These effects must not be resisted. So, for example, if we are impoverished or are born into a lower caste, we are working off the karma we built up in a previous lifetime. If we do not deal with the karmic debt in this lifetime, then we will need to in the next. One implication of this is that it is ethically questionable to relieve poverty and suffering in this world, since doing so condemns the recipients of our charity to suffering in their next lives.

In *other versions of Taoism*, karma influences your life in this world: wrong actions result in a shortened lifespan and sometimes direct retribution, as when a murderer is himself murdered. In this case, karma can be seen as the direct outworking of the *tao*, since failure to live according to the natural order has direct effects on a person's life. Unpaid karmic debt affects the doer's spouse and descendants until it is paid off, directly contributing to their suffering in this world.

Desire is another reason for suffering, particularly in Buddhism but also to some extent in Hinduism. In *Hinduism*, desire keeps us involved in the cycle of reincarnation. If we desire the pleasures of the physical world—which it is not wrong to do—we will be reincarnated so our *atman* can experience them. When we begin to desire the higher pleasures of the non-physical life, whether in the form of union with *Brahman* (ultimate reality) or as a servant of our preferred god, we can pass out of the cycle of reincarnation to the next world. In *Buddhism*, desire itself is the cause of suffering. Our cravings, whether for sensual pleasures or even existence, create attachment to this world, which causes suffering and produces karma. In the absence of desire, karma itself ceases to exist. But even the desire to escape karma is a trap that can create attachment to this world. In essence, then, every human desire, every pleasure or satisfaction we have related to anything or anyone in this world— even love—is the source of suffering; if we wish to avoid or end suffering, we need to purge ourselves of these desires.

It is worth contrasting Buddhism with Western thought on this point. Where Buddhism sees desires as being the problem, Western thought tends to think of them as the thing that makes life worthwhile. This is one reason why Buddhism and other Eastern ideas tend not to be adopted wholesale, but rather are mixed with Western thinking, resulting in New Age thought (see the next chapter).

Question 3: Is There a Solution?

Salvation is found in liberation from individual existence.

Although each religion has its own approach to salvation, they all revolve around eliminating ignorance and desire. In most of these religions, once you eliminate your ignorance of the nature of reality and purge yourself of the desire for existence, you see through the illusions that tie you to the world and recognize your oneness with all that is, whether that is seen as the order of nature, god, or non-being. At this point, your existence as a distinct, unique, personal being ends, and you are absorbed into ultimate reality like a drop of water into the ocean (or alternately, you cease to exist because existence itself is an illusion). So salvation means personal extinction.

In *Hinduism*, salvation can come in several forms, all of which involve the dissolution of the self (*atman*). In pantheistic and atheistic Hinduism, salvation comes from ending desire for existence in the physical world. This is sometimes coupled with attaining spiritual knowledge to eliminate the ignorance that leads to bad karma, with asceticism (rejecting the body), or with yoga or tantric sexual practices (using the body as a vehicle for attaining spiritual knowledge). Once enlightenment is attained, your *atman* (soul) is freed from the cycle of reincarnation and is absorbed into the impersonal *Brahman* (ultimate reality). You then cease to exist as a separate entity.

In theistic versions of Hinduism, liberation comes devotion to a particular god or goddess who is accepted as ultimate reality (*Brahman*). By performing the right prayers and rituals, we can either unite with or achieve a perfect and eternal relationship with the god. In this way, we are freed from the cycle of reincarnation and our *atman* enters deeper into *Brahman*.

In *Buddhism*, salvation is found through the Four Noble Truths: existence is suffering; suffering is caused by desire to experience existence; cessation of desire results in cessation of suffering; to eliminate desire, one must follow the Noble Eightfold Path. The Noble Eightfold Path includes:

- Right Perspective (i.e. seeing the universe as it is)
- Right Intention (i.e. ridding the self of desire)
- Right Speech
- Right Action
- Right Livelihood (i.e. not earning a living in a way which harms another)
- Right Effort
- Right Mindfulness
- Right Concentration

According to the Buddha, following the Noble Eightfold Path must be done by personal effort; no grace or other external help is available. By following this path, typically over the course of several lifetimes, it is possible to achieve enlightenment, a state in which you have eliminated all desire (and with it, the things we value as human beings) and see through the illusion that the physical world around us is real. This destroys whatever karma has built up in your mindstream.

Depending on the particular form of Buddhism, you either continue in this life as an *arhat*, an enlightened being, and then enter a state of non-being at your death, or become a *bodhisattva*, a celestial being who postpones personal extinction to serve as a guide to those seeking enlightenment. (The latter option is a departure from the Buddha's original teaching that enlightenment can only come from unaided personal effort, but it is part of Tibetan Buddhism and Mahayana Buddhism.) In either case, the ultimate goal is non-existence. It is neither absorption into ultimate reality since there is no ultimate reality to be absorbed into, nor annihilationism since there is no self to annihilate. It is simply the ending of the illusion of existence.

The difficulties involved in living within this philosophy are best illustrated by the Japanese poet Issa, who, after his beloved daughter died, wrote this haiku:

> The world of dew
> Is a world of dew, and yet,
> And yet....

In *Taoism*, liberation comes from discovering and living according to the *tao*, the universal law that governs existence. Learning to live according to the *tao* is achieved through the practice of *wu-wei* (non-acting), in other words, through learning to live effortlessly, spontaneously following the *tao* in all things. Union with the *tao* can come from physical and spiritual exercises, diet, psychedelic drugs, sexual techniques similar to tantric yoga, meditation, or a variety of other practices. These result in long life—some Taoists believe it is possible to become immortal through them—but the ultimate goal is to attain spiritual knowledge that recognizes instead that one is part of the *tao*, that life and death are simply different aspects of ultimate reality, and that personal identity is an illusion. So once again, salvation means the end of personal existence through seeing through the illusion that the world consists of separate entities.

Question 4: What is My Purpose?

The purpose of life is to reach enlightenment and so pass out of the cycle of reincarnation/rebirth and achieve liberation (i.e. personal extinction).

Most people are so far from enlightenment that it will take many lifetimes of consistent effort before it can be achieved. As a result, it is important to accept your karmic destiny (your lot in life) without complaint since you will need to work through that karma before you can advance (at least in most Eastern religions). In whatever state you find yourself, you must strive to build up positive karma to improve your status in the next life so you have a better chance of reaching enlightenment. Each religious system has a different group of practices that will help you achieve "liberation," as discussed in previous sections. In all cases, however, the problem is essentially one of perception: we buy into and desire the illusion of this world's existence rather than choosing ultimate reality, and thus we are tied to this world. The object is therefore to recognize and accept ultimate reality and to rid the self of desire.

There are a number of important implications of these ideas. Buddhist ethics frequently emphasize compassion, by which they mean an effort to end all suffering, in part because monism teaches that there is no distinction between you and the sufferer: compassionate action toward them is thus compassionate action toward yourself. Similarly, some forms of Hinduism emphasize selfless action on others' behalf, since there is no distinction between their soul and your own.

At the same time, salvation is always the result of individual striving, of learning either to see through the illusion of the world and to purge desire, or to live according to the *tao* or *dharma*. There is no concept of grace or of divine assistance (except for *boddhisatvas* in some forms of Buddhism). This means that there is nothing that you can do to help another with the consequences of their negative karma. Under these circumstances, what is the point of compassion or selfless action? It can't deal with the recipient's negative karma. Instead, it becomes a means to reduce your own attachment to this world and thus to lighten your own karmic load. Compassionate, selfless action is therefore a means to help yourself.

This also points to a paradox at the core of Buddhist ethics: if desire causes suffering, what about the desire to eliminate suffering? Does that also cause suffering? Ultimately, the answer is yes, just as the desire to become enlightened is a hindrance to becoming enlightened. Compassion, social action and the like must be done with complete detachment, otherwise the action reinforces the kind of desire that hinders spiritual development and delays enlightenment. This is hardly a strong motivation to take concrete action to relieve suffering.

Some Hindu thinkers take this even further. They argue that helping the poor, the sick, and the lower castes actually does more harm than good. Relieving their suffering in this life only condemns them to more suffering in the next since they will need to deal with their negative karma themselves at some point. Under these circumstances, it is no surprise that poverty is such a chronic problem in many traditionally Hindu and Buddhist countries: their worldviews do not provide a coherent rationale or motivation to deal effectively with human suffering.

6—New Age

The New Age movement is a combination of Eastern philosophies and Western science, especially quantum mechanics and neuroscience, all filtered through the lens of a postmodern rejection of absolutes. The basic idea is that there is an underlying reality out there generally described either as "spiritual" or as a kind of energy. Many practices can help you connect with this energy, including holistic health activities, meditation, occult traditions, European paganism, Siberian shamanism, native American spirituality, Eastern religions, yoga, tai chi, etc. And in true postmodern fashion, whichever practice or combination of practices works for you is fine, because ultimately they all lead to the same place.

As a system influenced by postmodernism, it is difficult to generalize about New Age beliefs, because some people who could be classified under this category will reject nearly any element that could be listed as a characteristic of the movement. With that caution, however, there are a few elements that are broadly shared within the movement. First, they tend toward *pantheism*—the idea that everything is god—which means that the individual is god as well. But while they emphasize the idea that we are god, they tend not to point out that the same is true of pond scum: it is equally divine with human beings in a pantheistic system.

Since everything is god, fundamentally everything is also the same thing, so we typically have a form of **monism** (the idea that all things are fundamentally one) as well. But while the system tends toward monism, Western individualism also comes into play. The New Age movement tends to emphasize personal spiritual growth and with it, spiritual power. Although in principle, this growth will lead to the realization of the fundamental unity of all things, there is much more of an emphasis on the individual than in Eastern religions.

Truth in the New Age movement is built on a combination of personal experience and authority. People within the movement engage in practices sometimes called *"psychotechnologies"* to develop their spirituality—an ill-defined term that is somehow distinguished from religion but never actually explained. These psychotechnologies can be nearly anything: physical practices like yoga, tai chi, or tantric sex; meditation; rite and ritual; magic, psychoactive drugs; chanting; drum circles .... The list is endless. The idea behind these practices is to induce some kind of "spiritual" experience, which the teacher explains in terms of the group's worldview. The experience is then seen as proving that the worldview is true. The problem is that experience is never self-interpreting. For example, it is possible to generate an altered state of consciousness by using breathing exercises. Is this evidence of "chi," a mystical glimpse of the fundamental unity of all things, or a physiological phenomenon caused by changed blood chemistry or a biofeedback loop? The explanation offered by the teacher may not in fact be correct, and so the experience by itself proves nothing.

This does not mean that people who want to avoid New Age thinking need to avoid, for example, martial arts, tai chi, qigong, acupuncture, or yoga. These practices can in fact be quite healthy and only become problematic when they become a vehicle for New Age or Eastern religious ideas. The physical exercises themselves are safe as long as the practitioner is mindful of whatever philosophical baggage may be packaged with them.

Question 1: Where Did I Come From?

Human beings are the result of a combination of biological and spiritual evolution.

Because the New Age is a hybrid of Eastern and Western thought, elements of both are typically brought together into the explanation for human origins. Biologically, human beings are a result of evolution following secular naturalism's explanation of origins. To this, New Age belief frequently adds the idea of spiritual evolution as well, that is, our non-physical self is evolving into higher forms of consciousness.

New Age thought tends to view the world and human beings within as an integrated whole. Concern for the environment is very common among (though not exclusive to) New Age thinkers, because human beings are seen as simply one part of the natural order. This leads to an emphasis on living in harmony with nature, which in turn leads to an emphasis on holistic health practices. This frequently begins with an emphasis on eating organic foods (for both health and ecological reasons), but extends toward various forms of "mind-body" exercise (e.g. yoga and qigong) and various forms of "complementary medicine," including particularly energetic or vibrational healing (e.g. reiki and acupuncture). While these and other forms of complementary medicine may in fact be effective for some people, the results are frequently used to support a worldview that sees everything as being fundamentally energy, but operating on different wavelengths. In this way, we reach *monism* (and frequently *pantheism*) through the back door.

Two things frequently follow from the New Age version of the idea that everything is energy. One is that we can control the energy around us through our consciousness—in other words, we can create our own reality through exercising our mind. This is the idea behind many of the ideas about visualization, the power of the spoken word, the "law of attraction," and other similar ideas. Again, some of these may work to some extent, but not for the reason that is often given to explain them.

Secondly, since the laws of physics state that energy can neither be created nor destroyed, reincarnation is frequently a part of New Age thought. Although there are quite a few variations on this, in the most common New Age interpretation of reincarnation, you are part of an energy and consciousness stream that extends multiple lifetimes behind you. Most New Age thinkers do not focus on eliminating desire to pass out of the reincarnation cycle as Buddhists do. Rather, they tend to take a more Hindu approach to reincarnation, focusing instead on the more pantheistic notion that we are all god, and the way to rise out of the reincarnation cycle (if that is what you want to do) is to realize your own divinity. What happens after this varies from teacher to teacher, but in most cases you can continue your existence to help others on their road to enlightenment as a being sometimes known as an "Ascended Master," similar to a Buddhist *bodhisattva*. We will cover this more in a later section, but first we need to examine why so many of us face problems in our lives when in New Age thought we are able to create our own realities and so should be able to eliminate our problems.

Question 2: What is Wrong with the World?

Sin and suffering exist because people fail to recognize their own divinity.

Different New Age groups identify different reasons for the problems in the world, generally drawing from both secular naturalist ideas about corrupt cultures and Eastern ideas of ignorance of the nature of reality. Of the two, it is ultimately the second—the issue of ignorance—that is the most important. We are unhealthy because we do not know the proper things to eat and the right way to breath and to exercise. We do not prosper because we see life as competition where one person wins and another loses in a zero-sum game, rather than recognizing that cooperation, creating win-win scenarios, is the route to success. Ultimately, since we are all one (*monism*), another person's loss diminishes me. Because of our unhealthy emphasis on competition, we do not live lives of benevolence and love; instead, we plunder the environment and exploit others, leading to dysfunctional cultures (generally understood as Western industrial capitalism). Some New Age thinkers introduce karma into the equation as well, so that those who are exploited will get theirs in the end, either in this life or in a future incarnation. In some cases, misfortunes in life are also blamed on bad karma from previous lives.

A more extreme version of this focuses on the *postmodern* idea that there is no fixed truth, and that what is true is what is true *for you*. In much popular New Age thought, this means that you create your own reality: your mentality creates the conditions that you experience in your life. If you think of yourself as sick, you are sick; if you think of yourself as poor, you are poor; if you think of yourself as lacking opportunity, you lack opportunity; if you think of yourself as trapped, you are trapped. Any problem you have exists because you have attracted it into your life by your thinking and your words. This may be a result of karma from a previous lifetime—you have inherited a negative mindset from your karmic stream which you need to overcome in this lifetime—or it may simply be something that has been imposed on you by your family, your religion, or your culture, all of which conspire to keep you in ignorance of your freedom and your power to create a new reality for yourself through changing your mentality. In essence, this change in mentality involves recognizing your own divinity through seeing the fundamental unity of all things (essentially making you a pantheistic god), and thereby gaining access to the infinite power that is available to you to shape your world.

The problem of ignorance leads directly to the kinds of social forces that cause exploitation of people and the environment, repressive political and economic institutions and policies, and the other problems within society. All of these are produced by systems dominated by a spiritual inertia which locks ignorance of human potential into the culture. As in most forms of *secular naturalism* and *postmodernism*, human beings are by nature good and even perfectible; the problem is not individuals but impersonal institutions even though these are also controlled by individual human beings. In the end, these problems will only end when there is a massive shift in the mentality of the peoples of the world, pioneered by enlightened people who realize

82

their own power and divinity, see through the illusion of ego distinctions to the underlying unity of all things, and thus find their way out of ignorance.

Question 3: Is There a Solution?

By using any of a number of spiritual paths, we can have the spiritual experiences that open our eyes to our own divinity.

Some thinkers argue that the New Age movement is not really a belief system but a collection of practices: various forms of meditation, magical rites and rituals, energetic medicine, past life regression, channeling, astral projection, shamanism, divination, yoga, martial arts . . . . The list is nearly endless and constantly growing. Yet what makes these New Age is not necessarily the practice itself—martial arts, for example, can be studied by soldiers or law enforcement personnel to help them carry out their jobs, not as a spiritual practice—but the reason or goal of the activity. New Age practices are intended to point the way to the emergence of a "higher consciousness" in the practitioner, to achieve a form of enlightenment that changes fundamentally your relationship to the world. In the vast majority of cases, this involves a new, generally pantheistic vision of the world and awakening or recognizing your own divinity as an expression of the great cosmic whole. As a result, the enlightened individual is serene, benevolent (since helping others is the same as helping yourself), full of peace, love, and harmony, as well as in control over the circumstances of life. One principle difference between the New Age and most Eastern religious systems is that most New Age thinkers believe that your consciousness continues after death and even after enlightenment: "liberation" understood as personal dissolution is not usually part of the program.

The New Age movement tends to be non-dogmatic about solutions. Since all roads (or at least many roads) lead to the same spiritual truth, it does not matter which path you follow. Eclectic approaches are quite common, as each individual chooses from a smorgasbord of options to construct a personal spiritual path. A Wiccan may practice tai chi (from Taoism), combined with yoga (from Hinduism) and Reiki (from Japanese Buddhism), but also participate in Native American chanting and dancing in Sedona, Arizona (to take advantage of the energy vortices there) or African drum circles, and receive past life therapy, all of which are seen as pointing to the same spiritual truth. Though not all New Age practitioners are eclectic, many are, and so New Age groups tend to be very good at networking since they share both practitioners and the ultimate goal of reaching enlightenment, and they view the successes and experiences generated by their practices through the lens of a common worldview.

Not surprisingly, the New Age movement draws its adherents primarily from the well educated, particularly those from upper middle class and wealthy backgrounds or aspirations. People who are struggling to make ends meet rarely have the time, resources, or inclination to pursue spiritual enlightenment or to spend money on the classes that lead there. The movement is thus a phenomenon centered on elites rather than the masses.

Question 4: What is My Purpose?

When enough people experience spiritual awakening, it will cause a revolution in consciousness on the planet, bringing in a New Age of peace, love, and harmony.

The New Age movement gets its name from the astrological Age of Aquarius, a promised "new age" where we will evolve into the next stage of human development. Led by spiritually enlightened people, both living and "ascended masters"—enlightened teachers who have already passed on to a higher state of life but who choose to instruct people on the road to enlightenment via channeling, visions, meditation, or other means—the world is gradually developing a new, higher level of consciousness. Thus "Indigo Children" born today are more spiritually aware and sensitive than children born in previous generations. When this new consciousness becomes sufficiently widespread, there will be a paradigm shift in human thought, and the new age will dawn. This new age is predicted in both Western astrology (the Age of Aquarius) and the Mayan calendar (though Mayan scholars reject this understanding of the calendar).

The usual explanation for the arrival of the new age is often called the "Hundredth Monkey Effect." As the story is usually reported, Japanese scientists studying macaques (a type of monkey) on one island observed that some of them began washing sweet potatoes before eating them. When enough of them started doing this, macaques on another island suddenly and spontaneously began doing the same thing. In other words, the skill transferred instantly from one island to another because of a change in macaque consciousness. The same thing will happen with humanity once enough people reach the enlightenment. Unfortunately, the story itself is mostly false, having been effectively debunked by Elaine Myers, Ron Amundson in *The Skeptical Inquirer*, and others.

In any event, the individual's purpose is to live in harmony with the world and with other people by being benevolent and loving, and to seek enlightenment or at the very least to advance along the road so you stand a better chance of reaching it in your next lifetime. By so doing, you are moving the world closer to the promised New Age, which is the ultimate hope of humanity.

7—Gaian Worldview

The Gaian worldview has its origins in the *Gaia Hypothesis* (now classified as the *Gaia Theory*) originally proposed in the 1970s by James Lovelock with support from Lynn Margulis. The Gaia Theory states that the Earth and the life on it are together a single complex organism that interact to maintain a stable environment favorable to life.

The theory can lead in several directions. At the most basic level, it simply means that living organisms affect the environment. The next step sees the Earth's biosphere as a self-regulating mechanism in which living beings interact with each other and with the environment to maintain the conditions for life.

From there, more radical versions of Gaia Theory move out of the realm of science into philosophical and theological speculation. These views see all life on Earth as part of a single being called Gaia, named after the ancient Greek primal Earth goddess. Gaia produces the environment (the Earth's crust, the atmosphere, the seas, etc.) through the interconnected evolution of the creatures that make up Gaia. A more extreme version of this idea sees Gaia as a single organism that consciously manipulates the climate to support life.

From there, Gaian Theory turns into a religious philosophy known as *Gaianism*, or *eco-spirituality*. Gaianism is influenced by both New Age pantheism and postmodernism. It effectively treats Gaia as a goddess and holds to a philosophy of honoring the Earth and treating all its creatures with respect, as well as working to reduce humanity's impact on the planet. Gaians often insist that Gaia is Earth's proper name, so that we think of "Her" in personal terms. However, in true postmodern fashion Gaianism is non-dogmatic, allowing it to be integrated with other religious and faith traditions including Buddhism, Hinduism, Daoism, Paganism, Christianity, and Judaism.

Although somewhat controversial, the scientific aspects of the Gaia Theory are widely accepted by scientists from a variety of fields. They are also the foundation to the programs of most environmental groups and activists. At this point, the scientific theory can turn into a worldview: when the health of the environment becomes the sole absolute ethical issue that colors how everything else is seen, Gaia philosophy has become the framework used to interpret all of life. Though details vary depending on whether the worldview is anchored in a scientific, philosophical, or religious interpretation of the Gaia Theory, the answers to the worldview questions remain the same. So although environmental scientists may dismiss the religious philosophy of Gaianism as nonsense, they may answer the basic worldview questions in the same way. If they do, they hold to a common worldview regardless of whether it is couched in scientific or theological terms. For purposes of this chapter, we will refer to this as the "Gaian worldview," whether or not it is connected to Gaianism as a religious philosophy.

Question 1—Where Did I Come From?

Human beings evolved from earlier life forms as part of an interconnected web of life in Gaia's biosphere.

Human beings are part of the environment, no different from any other creature. We evolved jointly with other living beings as part of Gaia, understood either as a tightly integrated environmental system or as a living organism itself. Like all other living beings, we are both part of the environment and shape the environment.

As part of Gaia, it is important for us to fulfill our proper function within the ecosystem, much like an organ in a healthy body has to fulfill its proper function for the good of the whole and for its own survival. As in secular naturalism, human beings are essentially no different from other animals, though unlike secular naturalism the Gaian worldview argues that our lives do have meaning: with all other creatures, our job is to preserve the biosphere, to perform our role in making Gaia fit for all living creatures.

The insistence that human beings are one part of the web of life, no different from any other living organism, leads among other things to the animal rights movement. To quote Ingrid Newkirk of People for the Ethical Treatment of Animals, "Animal liberationists do not separate out the human animal, so there is no rational basis for saying that a human being has special rights. A rat is a pig is a dog is a boy. They are all mammals." (*Vogue*, Sept. 1, 1989) Because there is no real difference between different species, in true postmodern fashion human beings cannot justly exploit or oppress other species. In fact, we must act to preserve the rights of living creatures, whether great apes (as in Spanish law) or plants (as in Swiss law).

At the same time, however, the very fact that people have these responsibilities indicates that we are in fact different from other animals. A tiger does not care if its next meal is an endangered species, and no one suggests it should; that we do care (or should) indicates that human beings are in fact different from other mammals. We are responsible for our actions and for the environment in ways that other creatures are not.

Question 2—What is Wrong with the World?

The world is in trouble because human beings have exploited Earth's physical resources, abused its creatures, and polluted the environment to such a degree that we are on the verge of causing catastrophic changes to the biosphere.

The Gaian worldview is unique among the non-Christian worldviews surveyed in this book in that it places responsibility for the evils in the world (defined as environmental degradation) squarely in human hands.

Other environmentalists who do not share this worldview, including many Christians, have long fought for responsible environmental policies, including an end to destructive mining and drilling practices, pollution controls, protection of endangered species, and so on. These can all be seen as important elements of Christian ideas of stewardship as part of the image of God. The key difference between these traditional ideas of environmentalism and the Gaian worldview is that for the latter, environmental protection is the ultimate good, and thus environmental degradation is the supreme evil. And there is no doubt in their minds that human beings, especially in the industrialized world, are guilty of damaging the environment.

And this evil is made worse by its extent. Human activity is not only responsible for pollution and environmental degradation on a local level; rather, we have done so much damage to the environment that we are rapidly approaching a tipping point beyond which recovery is impossible. Overpopulation consumes excessive resources and creates excessive pollution. Destruction of ecosystems leads to species extinctions, and that in turn creates imbalances that force nature to try to compensate to try to stabilize the environment. But the process can only go so far before it exceeds the earth's capacity to restore the balance. If we do not take immediate and drastic steps now, Gaia's feedback mechanisms will no longer act to stabilize the environment and protect life, but will instead spiral out of control to create catastrophic changes in climate and the environment.

The main threat we face today is generally believed to be anthropogenic (i.e. human-caused) climate change. Industrialization and fossil fuel use are releasing so many greenhouse gases, especially carbon dioxide, that Gaia cannot respond quickly enough to maintain climate stability. Greenhouse gases trap heat in the atmosphere, which will lead to global warming. In the short term, as Gaia attempts to compensate, we will experience increasing severe weather (*"climate chaos"*) until the greenhouse concentrations overwhelm the Earth's ability to respond. At that point, climate will shift definitively, resulting in rising sea levels, mass extinctions resulting from rapidly changing ecosystems without adequate time for species migration, and a host of other problems.

Catastrophic anthropogenic climate change is an article of faith in this worldview. Despite the fact that a substantial number of scientists, including prominent climatologists, are not convinced that the climate is changing due to human activity, nor that what has happened over the last century is outside the normal range of temperature variation, adherents of the Gaian worldview typically vehemently reject any challenge to their ideas about climate change. They instead argue that the case is settled science, beyond dispute and beyond discussion.

This response is, of course, non-scientific. All scientific theories are provisional, and the evidence in this case does not uniformly support the theory. Some adherents of the Gaian worldview admit that the data on climate change are not certain and that conflicting values shape the responses of scientists. On the other hand, if the theory of catastrophic anthropogenic climate change is true, the stakes are incredibly high and there is an urgent need for action. As a result, these theorists recommend shifting to *post-normal science*, which would bring in non-scientists who would be affected by the issue to develop an appropriate response to the threat. Critics object to this, arguing that it amounts to a politicization of science, imposes policies not supported by the evidence, and leads to silencing critics by accusing them of hidden biases. In response, supporters of post-normal science argue that the danger is too great and the issues too complex to rely on traditional approaches to using science to inform public policy.

Question 3—Is There a Solution?

Humanity, particularly in the developed world, must take immediate and drastic action to deal with environmental threats.

The immediate threat to humanity is catastrophic climate change produced by greenhouse gases; the obvious solution is to reduce greenhouse gases. There are two ways to this: we can find ways to take carbon out of the atmosphere by, for example, planting trees which convert carbon dioxide to cellulose; and more importantly, we can reduce the production of greenhouse gases, especially by drastically reducing the use of fossil fuels such as oil and coal, and replacing them with renewable energy sources such as solar and wind power.

There are a multitude of practical difficulties associated with switching to renewable energy. Transportation is a key issue, since electric cars are not practical yet and battery production is itself environmentally hazardous. Further, you still need electrical generation to charge the battery, and a great deal of electrical power is generated by burning coal. Solving these problems requires a massive investment of money into research and development, even if there is no clear prospect of profits. Since this won't be done by private industry, the government must step in with incentives, regulation, mandates, and funding to promote these technologies.

But since the problem is global, national solutions are not enough. International cooperation in the form of treaties such as the Kyoto Protocol is essential to protect and preserve the Earth. It is particularly important that the developed world, especially the United States, commit to reaching greenhouse gas targets while at the same time providing aid to the developing world to help them cope with the stresses caused by climate change.

The difficulty is that China produces more greenhouse gases than any other country in the world, and its production is growing far more quickly than any conceivable reduction from the U.S. or the E.U., yet the focus of most climate change efforts is on the West rather than China. Part of the reason for this may be practical: we can urge the Chinese to change, but we can actually affect policy in the West. But along with pragmatism, elements of "professional postmodernism" also enter the picture. The entire problem of pollution in general and greenhouse gases in particular is a side effect of industrialization, which was itself fueled by capitalism, which it is argued puts profits ahead of people and the environment. In other words, the environmental crisis was caused by oppression of the environment and of the developing world by the industrialized West. China, as a victim of this exploitation itself, is less to blame than the West, and as a result it is the industrialized countries that rightly must deal with the problems they created.

Frequently, the Gaian worldview also identifies human overpopulation as an important component of the other threats to the environment. More people consume more resources, release more greenhouse gases, and produce more pollution. Part of the solution is thus to reduce population, especially in the developed world where people use more and presumably pollute more. (Given the environmental conditions in many developing countries, it is an open question whether the West pollutes more than they do.)

Question 4—What is My Purpose?

My purpose is to live an ecologically responsible lifestyle and to work to save the planet through advocating for green policies in both the private and public sectors.

On a personal level, I need to adjust my lifestyle so that I have the least possible impact on the environment. There are a myriad of ways I can accomplish this. I can bike or take public transportation rather than drive; I can buy a more fuel-efficient or electric car; I can minimize driving and air travel; I can eat local, organic food; I can only eat free range meat or even go vegetarian or vegan so as to not oppress animals; I can recycle; I can compost; I can raise my own vegetables in my garden; I can buy Energy Star appliances, light bulbs, and high efficiency furnaces; I can insulate my house; I can set my thermostat to use less energy; I can have fewer children or none at all, since having fewer consumers is a good thing; I can support indigenous peoples by buying traditional crafts; I can avoid supporting large corporations, especially big box retailers like Walmart that crush local businesses; I can use alternative and complementary medicine so as not to support big pharmaceutical companies; and so on. Not all of these directly affect the environment, of course, but by expressing solidarity with native peoples and opposing large chain stores and major corporations we strike a blow against the capitalist ethic that leads to exploitation not only of the land but of peoples.

On a larger level, it is important to push corporations to be more "green" in manufacturing and distribution. Energy efficiency, biodegradable products and packaging, strict pollution controls, purchase of carbon offsets to absorb an equivalent amount of greenhouse gases as the corporation produces, "giving back" to the community through charity and volunteer services, all are important elements of the "green" corporation. We should reward companies that pursue these and similar policies, while avoiding those that do not.

But because corporations are motivated by greed and thus can't be trusted, it is important for the government to be involved to enforce environmental regulations. The Environmental Protection Agency needs to set and enforce stringent pollution controls, including for greenhouse gases. The government needs to subsidize alternative energies as well since they are not cost effective and cannot compete in a free market with traditional energy sources without governmental support. Along with direct subsidies for renewable energy, production of fossil fuels needs to be curtailed and taxed as much as possible to make it more expensive. If oil prices rise high enough, "green" energy becomes more competitive. Restrictions on drilling and on pipelines, particularly through designating key areas as protected wilderness not subject to development, will both limit pollution and make alternative energy more cost effective, at least in comparison to oil.

All of these are examples of tactical responses to the problems identified by the Gaian worldview. The key is that our purpose is to save the world environmentally, and this needs to be done by concerted action by private individuals, corporations, and government to avert the pending catastrophe.

Many of these policies and actions can be supported by people who hold other worldviews, of course. From the perspective of Christian stewardship, many of them are perfectly appropriate. But the question arises, is the danger to the environment so great that all other concerns are necessarily pushed aside to deal with it? In true post-normal science fashion, we need to ask whether in the face of the uncertainty about our imminent demise, should we turn away from other good things we could do to focus so single-mindedly on environmental concerns? For example, is environmental stewardship more important than the 250,000,000 people that contract malaria each year and the 1,000,000 who die from it, when the disease had been nearly eradicated decades ago, before DDT was banned? Is curbing greenhouse gases more important than providing clean drinking water in the developing world? If we can do both, why is so much energy spent on the former rather than the latter, which is much less expensive and easier to accomplish? Is reducing greenhouse gases worth the jobs it costs in the U.S., particularly when China's carbon dioxide production is outstripping the U.S.? Are people more valuable than animals? Is human trafficking a more or less serious problem than trafficking in endangered species? Do people in the developing world have a right to the kind of standards of living we take for granted in the West, and if so, how is that to be accomplished without producing more greenhouse gases?

On the corporate level, since many who hold to the Gaian worldview use the Internet, smart phones, GPS's, MP3 players, and other high tech gadgets, why are the companies that produce these exempt from the general condemnation of greedy corporations and environmental degradation? The GPS, for example, was created by the military and involves the space program. Are we concerned about the environmental impact of those organizations? What about the terrible conditions in the factories in China that assemble our high tech products? If we are really concerned about global environmental impact, how should we view that the environmental degradation in China caused by the production of the batteries that are used in our electric cars? If capitalism and development are so bad, why does the West have a far cleaner environment than the developing world and Russia?

To put it differently, it is difficult to hold the Gaian worldview consistently in our high tech world, and attempting to do so leads to a host of questions that pit human rights and lives against presumed environmental damage. While we should undoubtedly respond to ecological challenges, how we prioritize those compared to the value and quality of human life, particularly in the developing world, is an important question that too few people have thought through consistently.

Epilogue

You have just completed a quick tour of seven worldviews you're likely to encounter in America. Each one could be expanded and in some cases broken down into separate but related worldviews, but the overviews here will be helpful as you talk with people, listen to the news, watch movies, and generally interact with people and ideas in the culture.

Most people in the country hold to one of these seven as a base worldview, though they don't always follow it consistently. Sometimes they will incorporate elements of other worldviews into their own to deal with specific questions or problems; these ad hoc worldview syntheses rarely hold together well, though. It bears repeating: the introductions to the worldviews in this book are just that: introductions. The details may vary from person to person, and you need to understand *the person*, not put a label on the ideas.

Although worldviews tend to be stable, they do change over time. In fact, with the advent of mass communication and the Internet, ideas can be transmitted far more quickly and than ever before, with the result that we are seeing worldviews evolve more quickly than ever before. The New Age movement, with its hybrid East-meets-West outlook, is one example of this.

Looking Ahead

This raises the question of where these worldviews are heading. If these are the dominant worldviews today, what is coming tomorrow?

I'm a historian; I deal with the past. And I don't have a crystal ball that will tell me the future. But if I had to guess, I'd make the following predictions:

1. **Historic Christianity** is going to continue as an important worldview, though it is going to be challenged from two directions. From within America, the on-going split between liberal theology and historic Christianity will deepen, though the waters will be muddied by people who advocate social programs promoted by liberal Christianity but who maintain a foot in historic Christianity. My observations so far suggest that elements of the faith that have been accepted historically will be abandoned as needed to promote the social and political philosophies that this group supports.

   Another challenge comes from the spread of Christianity to the global south. As Christianity spreads to new cultures, it will take different forms, ask different questions, and have different emphases than historic (Western) Christianity. Some will see this as a challenge to the Faith, others will embrace it as a widening and enriching of the Christian tradition.

2. **Secular naturalism** will also continue, though as an intellectual force the New Atheists such as

Dawkins and Harris will become less influential as the weakness of their arguments is increasingly exposed. On the other hand, the militancy of the attacks on religion, and especially on Christianity, may increase as part of a reaction against the conservative social, economic, and political stances taken by vocal Christian leaders.

I think it is likely that secular naturalists will begin over the next generation to take more seriously the arguments about information presented within the Intelligent Design movement. How this will change the secular naturalist position is unclear, but just as it took a generation before the Big Bang was accepted, I suspect the same thing will occur concerning information theory.

3. **Postmodernism** as an intellectual movement is already dead everywhere except in education: it continues to be taught in universities, and teachers who were taught postmodernism continue to teach it in schools. The fundamental ideas are so incoherent that the rest of the world no longer takes it seriously

Postmodernism as a political movement will continue for the foreseeable future, however. It is a useful tool for promoting particular political and social causes that have powerful constituencies in American politics. Much of the shape of American society will be determined by the success or failure of ideological postmodernism.

4. **Islam** will continue to be a growing force in the world. Much depends on the nature of the largely Islamist regimes that came out of the Arab Spring. Though the majority of Muslims are not Islamists, the radicals are the loudest voices in the Muslim world by far, and thus they control the agenda. Religious minorities in Muslim states are likely to face even more pressure in the coming years, and conflicts on the interface between the Muslim world and cultures of different faiths are likely to increase. Islam will also continue to expand in the United States as well both by conversions and immigration. This will lead to tensions over the degree to which Sharia can be applied within Muslim communities, and over the proper relationship between Sharia and local, state, and federal law.

5. **Eastern religions** are seeing a resurgence in a number of countries in Asia, as more militant versions of Hinduism and Buddhism push for political power in some areas, and more strict versions of Buddhism look for converts. I do not expect these religions to have a major impact in America, however, since their fundamental outlook is so foreign to the way we think. Look instead for their ideas to be filtered to us through New Age thought, as has been the case up until now.

6. **The New Age movement** will continue, but its strongest cultural impact is now gone. It has

become largely a fringe movement with a relatively small number of serious devotees and others hanging around the edges. It will continue to influence culture in two ways. First, there will be on-going interest in "spirituality" (as opposed to religion) connected either to New Age psychotechnologies or simply to an awareness of some kind of supernatural reality behind the physical world. Second, media will use New Age related ideas in their plot lines and themes. Films and television will continue to promote fantasy and occult themes that can tie into the New Age, though there will be relatively few true converts to the worldview. People will dabble with the ideas and incorporate some of them into their base worldview, but I do not see the foundational ideas of the New Age movement getting much traction.

7. **The Gaian worldview** is likely to continue strong in the coming years. Although computer models that global warming advocates rely upon have proven to be woefully inaccurate in their predictions of global temperatures, faith in the models remains as strong as ever. Though some scientists argue that if we do not see warming within the next few years, we will have to abandon the model, the majority of supporters of AGW are publicly unfazed by the lack of warming.

If nothing else, legal structures identifying carbon as a pollutant and regulating its release will keep Gaian-inspired policies in place for the foreseeable future, even as developing countries release more and more carbon and developed countries fail to meet their targets. The end game here may be more about controlling the economy and developing alternative sources of energy than about climate change.

Among the general public there is increasing skepticism about global warming, perhaps because more people are more concerned about the economy than the ecology. On the other hand, there are enough other potential ecological fears to keep the Gaian worldview going for quite some time. Since at least the 1970s, there have been regular dire warnings of imminent ecological catastrophes, and though none of them have actually occurred, the movement has only grown stronger over the years. I see no reason to assume it will change now, though economic concerns may push it out of the mainstream of the culture.

Emerging Worldviews

This leaves the question, is there a new, emerging worldview on the horizon, something that will replace postmodernism? Undoubtedly there is, though the details are as yet unclear. One possibility is *hypermodernity*, which argues that things are changing and in many ways improving so quickly, that the history is no longer a reliable guide forward. Instead, we need to rely more and more on reason, with the goal of expanding personal freedom by transcending the limits nature puts on us.

For example, we can use genetic engineering to improve future generations by eliminating problems or enhancing abilities. Alternately, we can go the *transhumanist* route and create human/machine hybrids (e.g. using nanotechnology or genetic or cybernetic implantations) to improve our lives and even give us eternal life by downloading our minds into computers.

A second possibility is *supermodernity*. Supermodernity looks to overcome the postmodern deconstruction of knowledge by focusing not on truth per se, but on plausibility. Methodologically, supermodernity is built around an interactive experience of knowledge that allows you to chart your own course through the incredible wealth of information that is available online. The supermodern mindset combs through information and cobbles together a worldview or a system of ideas that seems plausible and thus can be accepted. This maintains much of the postmodern attitude (especially the freedom to define your own reality) while avoiding some of its logical problems by sidestepping the question of truth.

In some cases, this set of ideas then forms the foundation for a *tribe*, a cooperative, often virtual, community tied together by a common set of beliefs or practices, sometimes organized around a visionary leader. The tribe in turn often becomes a central part of the members' self-identity.

Whether or not supermodernity is the next big worldview, it does point to a simple fact about American life: the people you interact with every day may live in very different mental worlds than you do, with radically different outlooks, value systems, and ways of interpreting the world. Unless we can recognize and understand these differences in worldview, our ability to communicate effectively or to solve problems together will be severely restricted. Hopefully, this book will help you understand your neighbors and take the mental journey into their worlds to better communicate the Gospel and to deal effectively with the challenges we face as a society.

Suggestions for Further Reading

Charles W. Colson and Nancy Pearcey, *How Now Shall We Live* (Tyndale, 2004)

Nancy Pearcy, *Total Truth* (Crossway, 2008)

Nancy Pearcy, *Saving Leonardo* (B&H, 2010)

W. Gary Phillips, William E. Brown, and John Stonestreet, *Making Sense of Your World: A Biblical Worldview*, second edition (Sheffield, 2008)

James W. Sire, *The Universe Next Door*, fifth edition (IVP, 2009)

Steve Wilkens and Mark L. Sanford, *Hidden Worldviews: Eight Cultural Stories that Shape our Lives* (IVP, 2009)